YAR: ST

Scent &
Scent Bottles

Scent & Scent Bottles

Edmund Launert

Barrie & Jenkins
London

to Jean
for her patience, tolerance and help

© Edmund Launert

First published 1974 by
Barrie & Jenkins Ltd,
24 Highbury Crescent,
London N5 1RX

All rights reserved.
No part of this publication
may be reproduced by any
means without prior
permission of the publishers.

Designed by Michael R. Carter

ISBN 0 214 66905 X

Filmset by BAS Printers Limited,
Wallop, Hampshire

Contents

Chapter 4 Bottles in Materials other than Glass

Acknowledgements

For assistance in various ways the author wishes to thank the following: Mr. R. J. Charleston, Keeper of Ceramics, Victoria and Albert Museum; Mr. C. J. Elliott, British Museum (Natural History); Prof. F.-A. Dreier, Director, Kunstgewerbemuseum, Berlin-Charlottenburg; Prof. A. Geus; Herr Otto F. Ernst; Herr Wilhelm Henrich; Monsieur J. F. Costa, Director, Parfumerie Fragonard, Grasse; Monsieur G. Vindry, Curator, Musée d'Art et d'Histoire de Provence, Grasse; Mrs. G. Gros-Galliner; Mr. Leslie Scott; Dr. A. Polak; Mrs. Adrienne S. Wood, Houbigant Inc., New Jersey; Dr. Gisela Reineking von Bock, Kunstgewerbemuseum, Cologne; Miss M. A. Heukensfeldt-Jansen, Rijksmuseum, Amsterdam; Frau Karin Neubauer, Hans Schwarzkopf GmbH, Hamburg; Herr Georg Kunz and Frau R. Cervicek, Wella Museum, Wella A.G., Darmstadt; Dr. Hannelore Müller, Kunstsammlungen, Augsburg; Dr. Rainer Rückert, Bayerisches Nationalmuseum, Munich; Dr. H. H. Heine; Miss Alison Brand, Editor, City Magazines, London; the Director, Brighton Museum & Art Galleries, Brighton; the Director, Syndicat National des Fabricants & Importateurs d'Huiles Essentielles & Produits Aromatiques Naturels, Grasse; Frau Ingeborg Müller, Messrs. 'Farina Gegenüber', Cologne; Miss Nancy Graham; Commander Sir Hugh Dawson, Bt, CBE, RN, and Mrs. Maxine M. Baldry.

A particular debt of gratitude is owed to owners of private collections, who for obvious reasons wish to remain anonymous; they have not only made their precious objects freely available but also stoically endured the invasion of their homes by teams of photographers.

It is hard to find adequate words of appreciation for Dr. Bruno Storp, Director of 'DROM', Parfümöle für Kosmetik und Technik, Baierbrunn, for the generosity he has shown in making available numerous illustrations, all based on his own collection.

The line drawings were aptly executed by Miss Victoria Goaman.

Acknowledgements should be made to the following photographers: Herr Fritz Witzig, Munich; Mr. Peter Green, Imitor Ltd., London; Messrs. Mourré & Mayer, Grasse, and Studio Appollot, Grasse.

Introduction

PERFUME IN HISTORY

The origins of perfume are lost in the ritual smoke that rose at the earliest tribal or religious ceremonies. The very word is derived from the Latin *per fumum*, meaning 'through smoke', and the use of scented fumes is well documented not only for Roman society but for Far Eastern and Egyptian cultures also. The preparation of scented offerings was originally vested in the hands of priests, and the recipes were closely guarded secrets. In those remote times the boundaries between religious and domestic life were blurred, and perfume gradually began to play a greater part in the lives of the ruling classes. Living evidence of its religious use is provided in our day by the Roman Catholic Church, while its secular application is manifold.

Throughout its history perfume has been an expensive commodity and was prized by most of the famous and colourful characters in history. In Egyptian civilization Cleopatra and, more notably, Nefertiti used it lavishly. Vessels containing perfume and scented ointments were deposited in the tombs of Egyptian rulers and the story has it that sealed unguent pots emanated fragrances after more than 3,000 years when they were brought to light from the tomb of Tutankhamun. Many of the substances used are, of course, common to all the great civilizations. Egyptian perfume containers have survived, generally of glass and showing attractive combed patterns in various colours. Volumes could be written about perfume in the Egyptian and other ancient civilizations. Here a brief survey must suffice.

The Chinese and Japanese were familiar with and made use of aromatic substances. (The musk deer is native to China.) The inhabitants of the Indian subcontinent, whether Hindu or Muslim, used perfumes for personal and ritual purposes and supplied the Near East with woods, gums and herbs. Roses were beloved of many peoples and a Hindu noblewoman has the distinction of having discovered attar of roses, having noticed oily drops on the surface of a rosewater stream in her garden. The Persians were fond of rose water too, and elegant Persian rose water sprinklers (17th- and 18th-century examples) occasionally appear on the antique market. This delicate scent was made possible by the invention of distillation, supposedly by the Arab Avicenna, in A.D. *c.* 900. Hitherto perfume had been a combination of oils and petals which gave a strong but not always agreeable odour. Many useful plants grew in Arab lands: cinnamon, frankincense, myrrh, jasmine. Arab temples were pervaded by the perfume of musk and roses. From the year 1700 B.C. until the discovery of the Cape route by Europeans in the 16th century the Arabs carried on the trade in fragrant gums.

Perfume played no less important a role in Greek civilization. Theophrastus has recorded for us some of the plants used in perfume-making: cassia, cinnamon, cardamom, spikenard, balsam of Mecca, Aspalathos, storax, irisnarte, kostos, all-heal, saffron, crocus, myrrh, kypeiron, ginger-grass, sweet flag, sweet marjoram, lotus and dill. We are also aware that the Greeks liked the scents of violet, mint and thyme. The rose, the lily, the gillyflower and the quince were used in recipes. The pattern is the same as elsewhere: the burning of substances to sweeten the air, the use of ointments for the skin and of fragrant waters both for the person and for garments and furnishings. That the Roman enjoyed frequent baths is well known. After a bath he would be anointed with sweet-smelling oils in the appropriately named Unctuarium. Solid perfume, oils and, of course, rose water were known, and containers of the period such as the *aryballos* and variously shaped bottles in alabaster, terracotta and glass have survived.

The ancient Hebrews were familiar with the art of perfumery and the Old Testament is full of references. The New Testament mentions certain items: the offerings of the Three Kings come to mind, and the story of the alabaster box of spikenard. The circumstances of these incidents indicate the precious nature of the substances. Certain authorities maintain that the adoption of the Christian religion by Rome and its subsequent expansion throughout Europe led to the temporary neglect of the art of perfumery, except in ritual matters.

The Arabs continued to practice this subtle art, and later European contact with that people during the Crusades renewed interest in the West. Rose water was introduced into our culture by returning knights and was used, we are told, for rinsing the hands after meals—forks were a 15th-century innovation.

The rise of the guilds in Western Europe and the survival of their records enable us to bring a few specific dates into our narrative. For instance the London Guild of Pepperers and Spicers is mentioned in 1179 as dealing in all the above-mentioned substances. Perfume later passed into the control of the Apothecaries' Guild.

The earliest record of perfume makers and sellers in Paris is dated 1190, when they were granted a charter by King Philip Augustus, and there is evidence of a delight in rare and subtle odours throughout the 12th and 13th centuries. In 1268 the Glovers' Guild, operating from the Rue de la Pelleterie, was recognized. This guild struggled throughout the centuries to gain control of the entire perfume trade, eventually obtaining in 1614 letters patent to this end in which its members are described as '*tants maistres gantiers que parfumeurs*'.

Because of growing interest in perfume, France cultivated her native flowers to obtain extracts. These were sometimes incorporated with Eastern imports to obtain a scent such as *eau hongroise*, first made in 1370, which is the product of the distillation of cedar, rosemary and lavender. This is the first recorded alcoholic perfume; it was prepared by Queen Elizabeth of Hungary, who was reputedly so attractive as a result of using it that she received an offer of marriage from the King of Poland at the age of seventy-two! It is hardly surprising, with such stories current, that perfume was so revered.

The violet, the rose and all the blooms one associates with the flower fields of Provence were exploited at this time. Clothes and bed-hangings were sweet-smelling with lavender or some such fragrance. As in modern times, lavender sachets were put into drawers and cupboards, and more elaborate items such as the *oyselets de chypre*, and artificial birds impregnated with resins (storax, labdanum, besam, *gomme adragante*) were favoured. Orange blossom was also beginning to be appreciated as an invaluable source of scent.

The voyages of Vasco da Gama to Calicut, Goa, Malacca and other exotic places brought an influx of novel aromatic substances. The person and the table were invaded with strange new smells and tastes. The race to obtain these very desirable goods became known as the Spice War and was to last for two hundred years or more. It need hardly be pointed out that Italy was also indulging in the taste for delicious fragrances. Her interest in perfume had developed similarly to that of France: while Eastern goods were imported through the major trading-post of Venice, monasteries supplied the necessary herbs, and indeed the most famous Italian perfume manufacture was established by the Dominicans in Santa Maria Novella in 1508. With the rise of Italy's great families and their powerful influence on Western culture, the art of perfumery received more than adequate attention. Italy was supplying the rest of Europe with the finest perfumes, and was to do so until the 17th century, but the Italian and French skills had already begun to merge, on account of the arrival in France of Catherine de Medici. Let us for a moment, however, return to England, this time the England of the Tudors.

Henry VIII was fond of perfume and his son, Edward VI, is known to have composed a scent himself. (Perfume composing was to become a hobby of the aristocracy.) Queen Elizabeth, as every child knows, delighted in luxury of dress, and it is no surprise to learn that she also appreciated fine perfumes. Immensely proud of her hands, she was very pleased to receive a gift of gloves from the Earl of Oxford, and was even more pleased with their scent, which she henceforth referred to as The Earl of Oxford's perfume. Scent bottles of the period, used for sprinkling, were known as 'casting bottles', while solid aromatic substances were contained in perfume boxes, and these were considered an acceptable gift to make to Her Majesty. The *cassolette* (the name persisted into the 19th century) or *printanier* was a box in ivory, silver or gold pierced with holes to allow for inhalation, and there were also finger rings serving the same purpose. The court ladies enjoyed distilling their own perfume in the Queen's still-room and perhaps their interest was excessive, if we are to judge by a contemporary engraving entitled 'The Boat of Foolish Smells'. It depicts a boat containing an itinerant perfume seller and three silly ladies with asses' ears, one lady holding flowers, another a pomander, and the seller is shown with a series of pomanders threaded like beads hanging over his shoulder.

Elizabeth's contemporary, Catherine de Medici, obviously thought her perfumers indispensable, and Ruggieri and René of Florence therefore accompanied her to France. The latter opened up trading premises in Paris and became widely patronized. His royal employer was extremely interested in scientific matters but whether her rival, Diane de Poitiers, was equally interested in science, or was chiefly concerned with love philtres, potions and perfumes as means by which to enslave her royal lover, is open to question; she was at all events a connoisseur of perfumes.

Catherine has been accused, unjustly according to some sources, of being a poisoner. She is said to have brought the death of Jeanne d'Albret by means of perfumed gloves. At this point we should perhaps notice the connection between perfume and poison. It was believed that an odour could kill, and Gabrielle d'Estrées is said to have been murdered by means of a lethal scent which she inhaled from an elaborate filigree bottle.

During the Stuart period, the perfumed bath was much in vogue, and bags of sweet-smelling substances were worn on the person. (A perfume bag may be seen on display in the Victoria and Albert Museum.) Pleasure-loving monarchs or those with refined tastes naturally found a place for perfume at their courts. Charles II in England and Louis XIII and Louis XIV in France were notable patrons of the perfumer's art.

It was in the France of Louis XIII that many famous perfumes were created, such as neroli, the scent based on orange-blossom and called after the duchess of that name. This was the time when the perfume centres of Provence came into their own. The 'sweet-smelling monarch', Louis XIV, would personally supervise the compounding of perfumes, and as for the industry, this flourished during the period that Colbert was minister; perfume shops proliferated in Paris, and in Grasse an establishment that was to become famous was set up by Artand.

The court of the sensual Louis XV was known as '*la cour parfumée*'; there a different perfume was ordained for each day. Marie Antoinette was a devotee of perfume, and as for the king's mistress, Madame de Pompadour, her bills alone are evidence of her preoccupation with it. Two of her favourite scents were *eau de Portugal* and *huile de Vénus*. From this epoch dates *eau admirable*, and also *eau de botot* which was sold in flasks of reddish glass. But many less well-known toilet waters were also available, each presented with the manufacturer's distinctive label and packaging. The demand for perfume became frantic, and although attempts were made to extend the cultivation of plants used in perfume-making, the increase could not be met.

England recovered from the repression of the Commonwealth period and interest in perfume increased in the time of Charles II. In the 18th century the lavish use of fragrances of many kinds, and of cosmetics in general, became common. The vogue reached such a pitch that an attempt was made to restrain these practices by law:

> That all women [ran the Bill of 1770] of whatever rank, profession or degree, whether virgins, maids or widows, that shall from and after such Act, impose upon, seduce and betray into matrimony, any of his Majesty's subjects by the scents, paints, cosmetic washes, artificial teeth, false hair . . . shall incur the penalty of the law now in force against witchcraft . . .

Nevertheless, perfume shops were firmly established: Lilly's and Perry's in the Strand, and Bayley of Cockspur Street, operating under the famous sign of Ye Olde Civet Cat.

Across the Channel, poor Marie Antoinette paid the penalty for her love of luxury and lack of judgement. In the history of perfume she is remembered for her love of the scent of violets. We should not suppose, however, that luxury of this kind expired with her on the guillotine. Cosmetics continued to be used throughout the Terror, and what excesses of fashion there were at the time of the Directoire! The Merveilleuses and Incroyables, with their freakish dress, had a love of perfume as keen as that of any aristocrat of the Ancien Régime. Madame Tallien, the banker's daughter, sometime goddess of pseudo-religious ceremonies and wife of one of the dreaded emissaries of Robespierre, was regularly anointed with a perfume made to her own secret formula. Her implacable enemy, Napoleon Bonaparte, used two quarts of *eau de Cologne* a week and sixty flasks of Spanish jasmine essence a month. His Empress, Josephine, was very fond of musk and the headier scents, and these odours are said to have lingered at Malmaison long after her death.

Before leaving this period, the great French perfumer, Jean François Houbigant (fig. 1), should be mentioned. He lived from 1752 to 1807, and his career began in 1775 when, at the age of twenty-three, he opened a shop at No. 19, Rue du Faubourg St-Honoré, at the sign of the basket of flowers. Following the custom of those times, Houbigant worked as glover as well as perfumer. One of his bills, dating from the revolutionary year IX, tells us more of his activities:

> Houbigant, Marchand-Parfumeur, tient Fabrique et magasin de gants, Poudres, Pommades et Parfums, ainsi que le véritable Rouge végétal qu'il a porté au plus haut point de perfection. Il fait et fournit les Corbeilles de mariages et baptêmes avec assortiment complet.

> [Houbigant, merchant perfumer, manufacturer and purveyor of gloves, powders, pomades and perfumes, and also the genuine vegetable rouge

Fig. 1. François Houbigant
(1752–1807)

which he has developed to the peak of perfection. Marriage and christening baskets made and supplied, with full trimmings.]

The 18th century, with its inordinate desire for luxury products, was the ideal period to establish such a business. After the Revolution as well as before it those with means were only too eager to patronize the seller of scents, aids to beauty and novelties. Houbigant's bill of sale is evidence of this. It was made out to a Madame de Monbretton, and it shows that this lady was a frequent purchaser of all such delights. In a space of just over a year she seems to have purchased 29 pairs of gloves, 1 pair of men's gloves, a small amount of Naples soap, 3 pots of pomade, 1 pot of *cresme de roses*, 12 lbs of powder, 7 bottles of *eau de Cologne*, 1 bottle of *eau de jasmin*, 2 pots of *estrait double à la tubéreuse*, 2 flasks of *huille antique*, 4 bottles of *eau de miel*, and 7 bottles of *eau de bergamotte*. And I think we may safely assume that Houbigant was not her sole supplier.

Houbigant showed much acumen in installing himself in the Faubourg St-Honoré, then a new and very fashionable quarter of Paris. Indeed the quarter remains one of the most desirable and aristocratic in Paris. The type of building which housed his business is still to be seen, with tall windows, wrought-iron balconies on the well-proportioned façade and an open hallway or passage in the centre.

Houbigant's surviving accounts show that of all the toilet waters and perfumes he supplied, *eau de bergamotte* and *eau de lys* were his specialities. They also indicate that his illustrious clients paid well and without too much delay. Marie Antoinette was one of them, and there is a story that, on the very evening of the flight to Varennes, perfumes were being purchased for her at Houbigant's.

During the Revolution perfumes and cosmetics continued to be manufactured and purchased, despite the occasional attack from official quarters, and the names, of course, sometimes took on a topical note, as in *élixirs à la guillotine*. By the time of the Empire there was no longer any doubt about the propriety of such items. One of Houbigant's creations (for he was a perfumer in the true sense, and not merely a businessman) is mentioned by Victor Masson, who records in his *Souvenirs sur Sainte-Hélène* that 'deux pastilles d'Houbigant brûlaient dans la cassolette'.

In 1807 Armand-Gustave Houbigant succeeded his father, and built up a sound and flourishing business. The succeeding members of the Houbigant family were always at pains to preserve the traditions of the house, and remained at the same address in the Faubourg St-Honoré. In 1829 the 'reigning' Houbigant was appointed perfumer to Princess Adelaide of Orléans, which once again set the seal of approval upon the firm's activities. In 1838 he was appointed perfumer to the Queen of England and subsequently to many other European monarchs, including the Empress Eugénie.

With the advent of modern industrial methods Houbigant was quick to appreciate the implications. The manufacture of perfume was transferred from premises behind the shop to a small factory at Neuilly-sur-Seine, which expanded to become an enormous complex of workshops and laboratories. Trade is now carried on throughout the world, and the headquarters of this famous house are now in New Jersey, USA.

In Georgian England the aristocracy took an interest in perfume, though one would hardly suppose it was shared by 'Farmer George'. The name of his descendent, however, became a byword for luxury, gluttony and indulgence: the Prince Regent. His was, after all, the age of the dandies, and the royal perfume bills increased throughout the reign.

Queen Victoria showed no more than a decent interest in perfume. She favoured the English Essence Bouquet, whereas the Empress Eugénie of France preferred heavy, overpowering perfumes. These might have been provided by another celebrated perfumer of the period who should be mentioned here: Guerlain, the perfumer to Napoleon III. (The House of Guerlain is well-known to us today. One unusual feature is that it manufactures its own perfumes in Paris rather than Grasse.) When the French Second Empire was swept away and there was a revulsion from all its tastes, lighter, subtler fragrances were once more in demand. The perfumers of Grasse extended their repertoire more than ever before, and their products began to dominate the world market.

As the standard of living for the bulk of the population rose during the 19th century, scent ceased to be the exclusive enjoyment of the very wealthy. Eugène Rimmel, the prolific French perfumer who settled in England, recorded in his *Book of Perfumes* at the end of the 19th century, that there were about fifty manufacturers in London. Scent bottles, in consequence, were made in quantity and were of a humbler character, no longer the gem-encrusted, exquisite creations or porcelain delicacies of the 18th century. Most respectable Victorian ladies owned a scent bottle and it is these bottles, for the most part, that lie in our antique dealers' windows and which will form the basis of the modest collector's display.

The making of great perfumes has continued to this day, but the unique scent bottle is, alas, rare. Although commercial bottles are often attractive, they are to be found repeated in every chemist or drugstore throughout Europe and America.

THE SENSE OF SMELL

The attentive visitor to the Louvre will have seen and admired a most beautiful early 17th-century painting by Lubin Baugin, entitled 'Les cinq sens'. In this work each of the senses is represented by an everyday object, for instance, a mirror for the sense of sight. For the sense of smell the symbol is a bunch of carnations in a glass vase.

This is but one of many 17th- and 18th-century works, mostly still lifes, which have the five senses as their theme; a complete iconography of the subject would include works of art going far back into history. The sense of smell is almost invariably represented by fragrant flowers, either in bunches or as single blooms, and the pleasure derived from their scent is sometimes indicated by a figure holding the flower to his or her nose. Some of the most delightful examples of this are painted by Teniers. In some cases, however, the sense of smell is illustrated by a man smoking, as in 'The Five Senses' by Rombout in the Ghent Museum. Paintings of this kind may well make us wonder about the vital importance of the senses, and also about the value of each in relation to the others.

The senses of taste and smell are usually classified below the other three, sight, hearing and touch, and smell is often considered less important than taste. The traditional classification of the five senses is regarded by modern psychologists as a gross oversimplification, but we have long been aware, for example, of the interplay of smell and taste.

The taste buds on the surface of the tongue cannot identify certain tastes without the participation of the olfactory organ, although there is no anatomical link with the nasal membrane containing the olfactory receptors. Thus someone who has lost his sense of smell will not be able to distinguish—unless by the eye —between finely cut pieces of onion and potato. On the other hand the taste buds can distinguish, quite independently, between sweet and bitter, acid and salty. Our power of smell spans an infinitely wider range than our sense of taste. The main reason why the olfactory sense has no place in the arts is the fact that its mysterious effects on the human mind cannot be translated into any medium of communication. Whereas visual impressions (shapes and their relation to one another) and sounds can be defined, fragrances, in both quality and intensity, elude definition. And yet it is through our sense of smell more than the other senses that we perceive most of our unconscious impressions, many of them lasting a lifetime and often arousing profound emotions. The sense of smell has been of paramount importance to many a poet—to mention Baudelaire makes further comment unnecessary. Let me quote Joachim Ringelnatz, however, who wrote:

> In eines Holzes Duft liegt fernes Land,
> Gebirge schreiten durch die laue Luft,
> Ein Windhauch streicht wie Mutter deine Hand

We all experience that quickening of the memory when we recognize a scent or aroma first encountered years before. The memory for fragrances seems to be far more acute than for the sensations of the eye or ear. The faintest whiff of a certain scent immediately conjures up in our mind a vision of the scented object and perhaps its surroundings as well: a rose, a lily of the valley, freshly brewed coffee or, though 'scented' is not appropriate here, stables or a creosoted fence. Yet the process never works in reverse. The carnations in Baugin's still life, however realistically and beautifully painted, will not induce their fragrance in our mind; the painter could only present the flowers as a symbol. Paul Valéry described the smell of perfume as transforming the simple act of breathing into an intoxicating experience, but to express such an experience we have no means.

THE USE OF PERFUME

The real art of perfumery began to develop in the 15th century, though it was not pursued in a scientific manner until the 17th century and the liquid perfumes produced in the more enlightened times of the Renaissance, when the mediaeval fear of spirits and demons had largely been allayed, were not required to serve the same apotropaic purpose. Various sources have ascribed an aphrodisiac role to perfume but strictly speaking this is incorrect: aphrodisiacs always have the character of drugs, that is, they must be taken internally and, like most chemico-therapeutic measures, either have a direct effect on parts of the organism, in this case the uro-genital system, or achieve the same effect by stimulating certain glands, e.g. the hypothalamus. An impression registered by the senses of sight, touch or smell can only have a psychological effect, though this may in turn stimulate sexual desire. It is therefore much more appropriate to use the term erogenous when referring to the effects which perfumes are supposed to have *in rebus amatoris*. At this point it should be made clear that similar criteria apply to the whole field of cosmetics and good grooming, of which perfumery is an integral part; a well-chosen perfume will certainly prove more effective if complemented by a face enhanced by careful make-up and hair which has had the attention of a clever coiffeur.

The relatively modern science of behaviourism has not yet, to my mind, paid sufficient attention to the correlation between the human *vita sexualis* and the olfactory senses. We know of certain natural sex-lure chemicals in animals, the so-called pheromones, and quite recently a similar substance was discovered in a female rhesus monkey. The difficulty in establishing the erogenous effect of perfume on human beings lies, obviously, in the unreliability of any method, since we have not even developed an adequate language for the description of scents. It is not surprising that most research into this fascinating field has been conducted almost exclusively by psychologists; the number of relevant papers which have been produced over the last fifty years or so is quite impressive. The most important work to be published recently on this subject is Paul Jellinek's *Die Psychologischen Grundlagen der Parfümerie* (1965). As is the case with most psychological work, it has to be viewed with some reservation, but even without the revelations of lengthy research we are all aware from personal experience that our sense of smell, like all our senses, is instrumental in what is the main aim of all living organisms: that of propagating and thus guaranteeing the perpetuation of the species. There cannot be any doubt that the use of cosmetics, and this implies the use of all scented preparations, serves solely to attract the attention of the opposite sex. It is fascinating to note that almost all the ingredients used in the compounding of a perfume, whether obtained from the plant or animal kingdom, are associated with the sexual sphere of the organisms in question.

Throughout the history of man there has not been a single civilization which has not exhibited a highly developed art of cosmetics and perfumery. In modern Western civilization scent is used to complete an impression of hygiene, good grooming and affluence, as well as for its erotic effect. But no longer is it an integral part of domestic life and cultural manifestations, as in ancient cultures and as in some Eastern cultures still today. Much greater importance is attached to perfume in matters of love in the Orient, where the heaviest and most intoxicating perfumes are to be found, but since this narrative is confined to 'modern' European scent, the Oriental tradition in perfumery must be left aside.

As already stated, the sense of smell plays a much larger part in our life than we realize. It is said that the newborn child, with its undeveloped sense of sight, identifies its mother by the odour peculiar to her bosom. The body odour of an individual is complex, being composed of regional odours: there is a pronounced difference between the smell of the naked parts of the body and

Pl. I. Segmented pomander, silver-gilt and enamelled in the Mannerist style; foot and loculi set with table-cut gems. French, early 17th century. 90 mm high. *Parke-Bernet Galleries Inc., New York (reproduced by kind permission of H. Ricketts)*

Pl. II. Flacon or smelling flask, cut in aventurine, with hinged lid and silver mounts. German or French, late 17th century. 92 mm high. *DROM-Schatzkammer*

those covered by hair, and with the latter there are variations again, a head of hair having a smell different from those of the axillary or pubic areas. In view of this the Roman custom of applying different perfumes to different parts of the body seems less bizarre. Most people, however, are unaware of the extent to which they are affected sensually by any of these regional odours or their compound effect.

Body odours vary considerably according to the colour of hair and type of complexion, and several other factors, such as diet, play a part in determining the nature of an individual's odour. There can be no doubt that an over-emphasis on hygiene in recent history has greatly blunted our olfactory appreciation in sexual matters, and one cannot but deplore the present vogue for deodorizers which run counter to nature's intentions. Although initially attractive, body odour can subsequently become repulsive and this unpleasant smell, which is quite clearly anti-erogenous, is caused solely, in healthy people, by bacterial activity on the skin. Covering up this unpleasant smell by means of scent, results in a rather negative way in an erogenous odour. The erogenous effects of certain perfumes can be explained by the faint resemblance of their bouquet to body odours. This applies in particular to scents based on jasmine and jonquil, and some artificial compositions, all containing fixatives of musk, civet, castoreum or labdanum. But the stimulating effect of certain flower bouquets other than the few just mentioned is not always easy to establish: in many instances there may be a psychological explanation, since many flowers are type-cast in poetry and folklore, and thus the fragrance of a rose perfume will automatically arouse all the emotions symbolized by this flower. There are certain flowers, however, and therefore fragrances, which are becoming to a young woman but impossible for the ageing matron, and so one will associate the rose with youth and love and the camellia with fragile age.

Certain types of *eau de Cologne* with a predominant neroli note are regarded as pronouncedly anti-erogenous, while other flower scents—colognes with a predominant bergamot note, lavender waters or perfumes based on freesia, blue lilac and lavender—seem to have a tranquilizing effect.

In certain heavy scents (e.g. rose, heliotrope or hyacinth) the effect may be simply a narcotic one, the seductive powers of these scents being based not on erotic stimulation but intoxication, which lends to a momentary disturbing of natural inhibitions. To what extent these phenomena are caused by olfactory perception or by a direct reaction in the central nervous system through inhaling is not yet properly understood.

COLLECTING SCENT BOTTLES

To provide the collector with an exhaustive catalogue of scent bottles and containers is not the aim of this book, and in view of the enormous quantity of examples extant, to do so would be both impossible and undesirable. The serious collector will, in any case, be much more interested in understanding the historical, sociological and artistic background of the objects in his collection than in accumulating a great number. How was a certain scent bottle or container used originally, how has the craftsman adapted the object to the nature of the substance it was to contain, what does the character of an object tell us about its probable owner and the period in which it was made—it is the discovery of answers to questions such as these that gives the collector the greatest satisfaction.

He will find, for instance, that the nature of scent has governed the design of scent bottles: since scent is very volatile bottles were designed to be air-tight and impervious to light. And since all kinds of scent were invariably very costly, at least until the 19th century, bottles and other containers were made to be worthy of their contents.

Pl. III. Potpourri vase and cover encrusted with floral swags; upper part and cover pierced; panels with Watteauesque scenes enclosed by scroll-borders. German (Meissen), c.1755. 135 mm high. *DROM-Schatzkammer*

There is, unfortunately, no museum of perfume and its history to be found in Europe, not even in the very centre of perfume-making, the enchanting town of Grasse. There have been many celebrated perfumes in the past; their names are known to us but their bouquets are lost for ever, since no one thought to preserve them for future generations. (It would seem, also, that no provision has been made for creating a 'perfume-bank' in which to store the fine creations of the 20th century.) All that is left is the empty bottles, now in museums and private collections all over Europe, and we can only imagine the scent they once contained and the pleasure it gave to their gentle owners. These bottles are often of great human interest, as well as being sources of aesthetic pleasure.

Public collections of any note are rare. There are two museums with permanent collections devoted to the history of cosmetics, which, of course, cannot be separated from the history of perfumery; these are the Wella Museum in Darmstadt and the Schwarzkopf Museum in Hamburg. Both, as their names suggest, are privately owned by cosmetic manufacturers. The firm of DROM in Baierbrunn, near Munich, owns a fine collection of scent bottles from which many of the examples in this book have been taken. This collection, unlike the two just mentioned, is not open to the public but the owner will always admit those genuinely interested.

Fine specimens will be found, in this country, in the Victoria and Albert Museum (Schreiber Collection, inter alia), the British Museum, the Wellcome Medical Historical Museum (not always on view), the Castle Museum, York, the Royal Scottish Museum, Edinburgh, the London Museum, the Bristol Museum and many other provincial museums. Needless to say the scent bottles in private collections, in this country of collectors, far outnumber those in public museums.

In France one should visit the Musée des Arts Décoratifs, the Musée du Louvre and the Musée Cognac-Jay in Paris, the Musée National de Céramique, Sèvres, the Musée des Arts Décoratifs, Bordeaux, the Musée des Arts et d'Histoire de Provence in Grasse and the private museum of the Parfumerie Fragonard nearby.

Besides the specialized German museums already mentioned, the Bayerisches Nationalmuseum, Munich, and the Germanisches Nationalmuseum, Nuremberg, and many local museums, contain scent bottles and pomanders, and small museums are maintained by the firms of Farina Gegenüber and *4711*, both in Cologne.

In this book I have tried to include at least one example of every type of European scent bottle or container, and to place it against a backcloth of the history of applied art and social custom. As to the question of provenance, apart from indicating the country of origin or the major centre of culture or manufacture, I have not attempted to go into academic arguments, for instance, concerning factories. Likewise, only the names of great innovators or ingenious artists have been mentioned.

Perhaps it is not necessary to remind the reader of this book that each individual specimen was once owned and used by a person or a whole series of persons; indeed the identity of the owner may be the main attraction of a particular piece. How delightful to know that a piece may have rested in the hand of Madame de Pompadour or the Empress Josephine! These charming *objects de vertu* form a link with the past, and those readers who are not interested in aspects of technology or art history may nevertheless appreciate their intrinsic beauty and perhaps reflect on the shades of their long-deceased owners.

Chapter 1
Scent

RAW MATERIALS AND THEIR PREPARATION

The perfumer's raw materials are derived from the plant kingdom and also, though to a much lesser extent, the animal kingdom. From plants come essential oils, gums and resins. In addition, synthetic substances are playing an ever-increasing role in the perfume industry.

Essential oils are fragrant substances of various chemical compositions which have certain physical properties in common: they are volatile, soluble in alcohol and other solvents, usually colourless in the fresh state and, unlike fixed oils, they do not leave a permanent mark on paper. They are formed within the cells of the plant's tissue and may be contained within:

(a) the entire plant (e.g. lavender, verbena, mint, sage, rosemary)
(b) the flower (e.g. rose, jasmine, violet, carnation, jonquil, tuberose, acacia, orange blossom [neroli])
(c) the leaves and stem (e.g. geranium, bay, orange and bergamot [*petit grain*])
(d) the roots or rhizomes (e.g. angelica, vetiver, orris, ginger)
(e) the fruit (e.g. vanilla, nutmeg, caraway, aniseed)
(f) the rind (e.g. lemon, bergamot, orange)
(g) the wood (e.g. cedar, sandalwood, pine, rosewood)
(h) the bark (e.g. cinnamon, cascarilla [Croton elutheria])
(i) lichens (oak moss).

Out of 250,000 known species of flowering plants, only a small number (less than 2,000) contain essential oils; they belong to families scattered all over the system of flowering plants and are thus in the main not related one to another.

Each essential oil, and this applies also to perfume, consists of three 'notes' corresponding to three phases recognized by the perfumer: the top note (*note de tête*), the middle note (*note de cœur*) and the end note (*note de fond*). The top note is discernible when a flacon is opened and disappears shortly after the perfume has been applied to the skin. Top notes are usually caused by essential oils derived from lemon, orange or bergamot; their rapid evaporation is responsible for the refreshing effect of *eau de Cologne*. The fragrance emitted by the perfume when it has dried on the skin is termed the middle note and, as the French term so aptly implies, it is this phase which characterises a perfume. The end note determines the staying power of a perfume, that is, its ability to diffuse fragrance over a long period. It is governed by the right choice of fixative, one of the most trying of the perfumer's tasks, since most fixatives have their own aromas.

To the question 'How are essential oils formed in the plant?' scientists give conflicting answers, peppered with chemical formulae which I do not propose to inflict on the aesthetically orientated reader of this book. As to their purpose, that is, whether they are waste-products or intermediate stages in certain life processes of the plant, this remains as yet unsolved. There are indeed a number of problems in perfumery which continue to baffle the scientist. For a long time it has been known that the scent quality of an essential oil from a single species varies greatly from area to area, a fact which must be attributed not only to climatic conditions but also to the constitution of the soil or even the water. As every perfumer knows, there is no better absolute of jasmine oil than the one extracted from plants of the Grasse district, though the plant may be cultivated in many parts of Asia, Europe and North Africa. The most curious representative of this phenomenon is the bergamot: this thin-skinned, bitter, hybrid citrus fruit, whose complex parentage nobody really knows, is confined to a small area, hardly more than twenty square kilometres, in Calabria. The trees thrive here on irrigated chalky soil under incessant sunlight but always exposed to sea air, which ensures that the temperature is not too high. All these factors are well known and have been studied by generations of horticulturalists and perfume producers, but whenever attempts have been made to cultivate the plant elsewhere under similar conditions, it refuses to co-operate. Cultivation has been tried in Japan, Formosa, America and in the Ivory coast, but Calabria still holds the monopoly.

The essential oils are obtained from plant materials by various methods, the choice of which is determined by the nature of the plant itself. They are as follows:

Expression This method is used chiefly for the rind of orange, lemon and bergamot. In the oldest and least economic method the peel was either rubbed against an iron grater, or, having been softened in water, squeezed into bowls from which the essential oils were sponged out. Nowadays the process of crushing the peel is mechanised and the essential oils separated off by means of a centrifuge.

Enfleurage This has been the time-honoured method, and in many ways it is the best process for obtaining essential oils of high quality from certain flowers, especially jasmine and tuberose, which continue to produce essential oils long after they have been gathered. Since no heat is involved, the rather delicately balanced chemical composition of the essential oils is not disturbed in the process, which is based upon the principle that essential oils dissolve into fats. The fat, a mixture of beef fat, lard and gum benzoin, is spread on to both sides of glass panes mounted in wooden frames or 'chassis'. The freshly picked blossoms are pressed on to the fat where they remain until their essential oils have been absorbed by the fat, a process which may take from one to three days. The flowers are then removed and replaced by fresh ones, this routine being repeated until the fat is saturated with essential oils. The resulting unguent is known as pomade. In order to free the essential oils the pomade is treated in a solvent, usually alcohol, which takes up the essential oils but not the fat. A subsequent cooling of the solution to below − 10°C. causes the remaining traces of fat to solidify, making their removal easy. The essential oils are then separated from the solvent by means of distillation, and the resulting products are known as enfleurage absolutes. As far as I know enfleurage was confined to the perfumeries of the Grasse area. The process is unfortunately both tedious and time-consuming and, in view of labour costs, no longer an economic proposition. At the time of writing enfleurage is practised by only one of the Grasse perfumeries, and on a minute scale for prestige purposes only.

Maceration The principle is the same as that of enfleurage, but in this process the flowers are immersed in fat of a temperature around 65°C. When saturated, the fat (or oil) is cooled and subjected to a treatment similar to that described for enfleurage.

Extraction by solvent This is only used as a rule for very delicate flower material, and it was first applied by Robiquet in 1835 for the extraction of the essential oils of jonquils. The flowers are washed in a volatile liquid which, in view of the detrimental effect of heat on scent, must have a low boiling point, e.g. petroleum ether, acetone, benzoin, toluene or butane. The flowers are placed on sieve-like metal trays contained one above the other in large cylindrical metal tubes through which the solvent passes in a downward flow. The process is repeated until the flower material is exhausted of its fragrant products. The solvent is then evaporated and recovered, and the essential oils are left behind within a mixture of insoluble plant waxes, termed the *concret*. The essential oils are then extracted by treating this mixture with alcohol after the solution has been cooled to about −20°C. The absolutes are finally obtained by distilling off the alcohol. Although quite an important method, extraction by solvent is an extremely expensive one. A much cheaper and therefore more widely used method is distillation in steam.

Distillation in steam The history of this process goes back, supposedly, to Avicenna. For various reasons, one being the heat involved, not all aromatic plants can be subjected to it. It is most commonly applied to lavender, ylang-ylang, rosemary, patchouli and bergamot. The underlying physical principle of distillation is well known, but it should be mentioned that in larger factories the process is carried out under vacuum to keep the heat below a damaging level. Distillation on an industrial scale can only take place in areas where a constant supply of fresh plant material is available in sufficient quantities to justify the installation of expensive machinery. These conditions are satisfied in the bergamot area of Calabria, in the Valley of Roses in Bulgaria and, of course, in southern France, most notably in Grasse and its environs. There are, however, a few small stills operated on farms by a handful of workers, both in Europe and further afield. Many flowers have to be processed instantly, since they lose their fragrance shortly after picking, a fact which puts lengthy transport out of the question. In some cases the still is only in operation during the short flowering period each year—indeed some years it may not be used at all owing to unfavourable weather. As mentioned earlier, plant species growing in different soils produce essential oils of different quality, and therefore many a grower prefers not to pool his superior product with that of his neighbours; in some areas, however, and especially in North Africa, peasants form co-operatives to use a communal still.

Essential oil produced in these primitive stills cannot as a rule be used by the modern perfumer until further refined. This is achieved by a number of processes known in the chemist's jargon as rectification, 'dry distillation' in a vacuum and fractionation. The machinery used in all these operations is a far cry from the paraphernalia of the classical perfumer. Without going into detailed descriptions of these modern devil's kitchens, it is enough to say that some essential oils, taken as they are produced by the plant, can be separated into several fractions, each of which has its own character and can be used for a particular end by the perfumer.

This brief survey of the five methods of producing essential oils should help to explain to the reader why the final product, that is, the perfume we buy bottled, sealed and packaged in such small quantities, is so expensive. Nevertheless, the cost of machinery and labour make up only a small proportion of the total. This becomes apparent when we consider the amount of flower material involved.

The amount of essential oils contained in plants varies considerably from species to species, but even in the most extreme case the yield of oil makes up only a tiny fraction of the plant's substance. To give only a few striking examples: in order to achieve a yield of one kilogram of absolute oil of each kind one needs 725 kg. of jasmine flowers, 700 kg. of rose petals (the equivalent of a quarter of a million individual petals!), 1,000 kg. of orange blossoms, 1,000 rinds of bergamot fruit and almost 2,000 rinds of lemon and orange. Flowers are invariably picked by hand, and the labour costs involved are very considerable. A skilled worker in the Grasse area can pick between 4,000 and 5,000 jasmine flowers an hour, but this must be done before dawn. Certain flowers such as jasmine, must be harvested before the sun touches them, and processed immediately. The essential oil of orris root is extremely costly. The oil forms within the rhizome, but the plant material must be stored for several years before the oil can be extracted. No wonder that the price per kilogram of absolute of orris ranges from £1,000 to £1,700.

Finally, figures for the total amount of plant material processed annually at Grasse alone (based on the 1970 statistics) may give pause to anyone who buys a bottle of perfume: tuberose 4,000 kg., jasmine 314,000 kg., rose 360,000 kg., orange blossom 359,000 kg., jonquil 16,000 kg., lavender 6,400 metric tons!, and lavindin 122,000 metric tons. The products from the animal kingdom, by comparison, are no less expensive: 25 grams of musk can cost between £20 and £30.

Plant Sources Of all the plants producing essential oil, only a relatively small number are of economic importance in perfumery.

That which springs first to mind is the 'queen of flowers', the rose, of which certain species (Rosa centifolia, R. damascena (fig. 2) and R. alba) are cultivated in Europe, chiefly in Bulgaria and the South of France. During the flowering period (April to July) the flowers are hand picked in the late bud stage and taken immediately to the area distilleries where the rose oil, also known as otto of roses or attar of roses, is produced. Owing to its narcotic effect the fragrance of the rose is one of the most erotically stimulating of perfumes.

The bitter orange tree (fig. 3) is the source of three different essential oils. The blossoms yield the costly 'orange flower absolute' as well as the less expensive neroli oil which should not be confused with the oil of orange obtained from the peel of the fruit; both the leaves and twigs yield oil of *petit grain*. Although the tree flowers twice a year, usually only the spring flowers are used for the production of neroli oil. Its main use is in *eau de Cologne*, giving a refreshing effect by its rapid evaporation. The oil of bergamot is similar, though it has a slightly narcotic component. As mentioned earlier, it is obtained from the bitter fruit of a citrus tree cultivated only in Calabria (fig. 3). Like neroli, it is used in *eau de Cologne*, and is also widely used in modern perfumes, especially those of the *chypre* type.

Perhaps even more important than the oil of roses and the above-mentioned citrus products—and lemon (fig. 3) should also be noted as a source of essential oil since it is often used in perfumes, soaps and cosmetics—is the absolute of jasmine (fig. 4): there is hardly any perfume of quality which has not at least a trace of it. When alone it may be described as heavy and stimulating, but in composition it rounds off a perfume without dominating it. Not infrequently, jasmine oil functions as a counter-balance to attar of roses in certain perfumes. Although native to southern Asia, jasmine is widely cultivated in Italy, Corsica, Egypt, Algeria, Morocco and southern France (around Grasse), but the oil obtained from Grasse is held to be of unrivalled quality. As is the case with rose oil, modern chemistry has not yet been able to produce a satisfactory synthetic substitute for the absolute of jasmine.

A natural product which is often used as a substitute or extended for rose oil in less expensive perfumes (although used for its own merits also) is geraniol, which is the main constituent of geranium oil and obtained from plants belonging to the genus Pelargonium (fig. 5). For perfumery purposes some of its fragrant species (P. graveolens, P. odoratissimum, P. roseum, P. fragrans and P. capitatum) are extensively cultivated in North Africa and southern Europe. The most significant characteristic of geranium oil is that its top note is faintly reminiscent of the smell of the pubic area of the blond-haired type.

The natural oil of violet, owing to its prohibitive cost, is nowadays entirely substituted by either the synthetic ionone or by orris. Violet flowers (fig. 6) contain only a minimal amount of essential oils, and their gathering is an extremely tedious job. At the beginning of this century, when cheap labour was still available, hectars of violets were cultivated in the South of France, usually under olive trees, for the perfumeries of the region. Violet-scented perfume, although regarded as old-fashioned today, has always evoked people's emotions; it has a narcotic effect and a slightly heady note, and its erotic nature is undeniable.

Orris is obtained from the rhizomes of several Iris species (but mainly from I. germanica) which are cultivated for this purpose throughout the Mediterranean region and is of great value to the perfumer. Besides the violet-like scent, its most important characteristic is its subtle similarity to the smell of the natural oils of the hair.

The use of lavender in perfumery has a long history going back to Roman times. For the English reader this particular plant evokes memories of lavender sachets and the lavender stick (fig. 7) to be found in wardrobes and linen chests in almost every household two or three generations ago: it was not only its pleasant, soothing fragrance but also its moth-repellant qualities which made this herb so popular. Lavender water has been employed since Elizabethan times and many country mansions had their own stills for its production. Lavender-scented powders, soaps and other cosmetic preparations made by old established firms such as Yardley or Floris have made the fragrance of English lavender well-known all over the world.

Despite a climate decidedly unfavourable towards essential oil-yielding plants, lavender of high quality was grown on a large scale in England, mainly in the Mitcham area, right up to the beginning of this century. There are 19th century engravings of extensive lavender fields with the Crystal Palace in the background.[1] With the exception of a few pockets in Norfolk and the South of England, lavender distillation is today carried out exclusively in France. Of the many species of this large genus of the mint family only two are of commercial interest. Common lavender (Lavandula officinalis, fig. 8) grows in mountainous regions (between 1,000 and 2,000 metres) in southern France (Haute Provence, parts of the department of Vaucluse and the Dauphiné). About ninety-five per cent of the world's supply is produced here, from wild as well as cultivated plants. Another species, known as spike lavender (L. latifolia), which grows at lower altitudes of the same regions (up to about 850 metres), yields a less expensive oil. The natural hybrids between these two species, the so-called lavandins, are of great importance in the production of essential oils for soap and cosmetic preparations; the production of lavandin is, incidentally, eight to ten times greater than the amount of oil available from common lavender.

The mint family comprises a relatively large number of aromatic herbs. Rosemary (fig. 9) and thyme (fig. 10), less important than lavender, are also used for perfume and scented soaps. And there is one exotic herb, patchouli (fig. 11), which is grown mainly in Malaysia and Sumatra. Patchouli, with its heady note, has the reputation for being one of the most erotic of all perfumes: no wonder that there is a great vogue for it at the moment among the Carnaby Street clientele. Many of the perfumes sold cheaply under this name do not, however, merit the attention of discriminating users. Patchouli is valued not

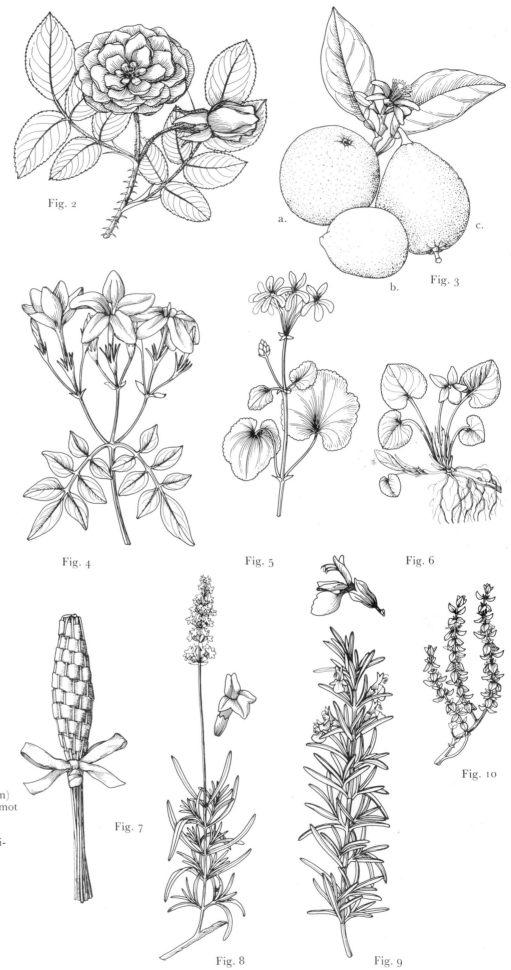

Fig. 2

Fig. 3

a.

b.

c.

Fig. 4

Fig. 5

Fig. 6

Fig. 7

Fig. 8

Fig. 9

Fig. 10

Fig. 2. Rose (Rosa damascena)
Fig. 3a. Orange (Citrus aurantium)
b. Lemon (Citrus limon) c. Bergamot
—flowering branch and fruit—
(Citrus aurantium var. bergamia)
Fig. 4. Jasmine (Jasminum grandi-
florum)
Fig. 5. Geranium (Pelargonium
odoratissimum)
Fig. 6. Violet (Viola odorata)
Fig. 7. Lavender stick
Fig. 8. Lavender (Lavandula
officinalis)
Fig. 9. Rosemary (Rosmarinus
officinalis)
Fig. 10. Thyme (Thymus spec.)

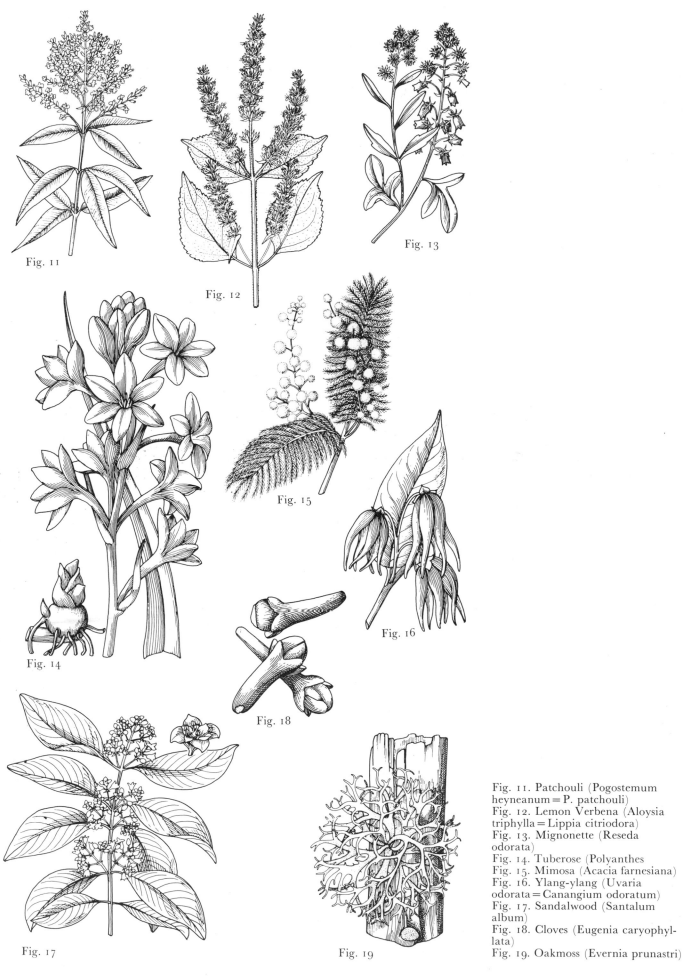

Fig. 11

Fig. 12

Fig. 13

Fig. 14

Fig. 15

Fig. 16

Fig. 18

Fig. 17

Fig. 19

Fig. 11. Patchouli (Pogostemum heyneanum = P. patchouli)
Fig. 12. Lemon Verbena (Aloysia triphylla = Lippia citriodora)
Fig. 13. Mignonette (Reseda odorata)
Fig. 14. Tuberose (Polyanthes
Fig. 15. Mimosa (Acacia farnesiana)
Fig. 16. Ylang-ylang (Uvaria odorata = Canangium odoratum)
Fig. 17. Sandalwood (Santalum album)
Fig. 18. Cloves (Eugenia caryophyllata)
Fig. 19. Oakmoss (Evernia prunastri)

25

only for its own fragrance but also, and more highly, for its quality as a fixative of fine perfumes, mainly those of the *fougère* complex. Readers of the older generation may still remember the fragrance which emanated from cashmere shawls subtly scented with patchouli.

Another exotic herb, lemon verbena (fig. 12), is native to Peru and widely cultivated in Algeria and the South of France: its essential oil forms a base for colognes. Mignonette (fig. 13), however, is native to the Mediterranean area; its essential oils, obtained by extraction by solvent, do not have the stimulating fragrance of the original flower, the faintly sweaty aroma of which has therefore to be recreated by the perfumer. Grasse is the main centre for cultivation of the tuberose (fig. 14), a member of the Amaryllis family. Its beautifully waxy white inflorescences appear between July and September, and are snipped off early in the morning and processed immediately. The heavy bitter-sweet aroma of its flowers is famed for its aphrodisiac properties which almost rival those of jasmine. Whereas in jasmine the erogenous effect is caused by a note faintly reminiscent of faeces, in the tuberose it stems from a sweaty, acrid characteristic.

The plant commonly known as mimosa in perfumery actually belongs to the genus Acacia (fig. 15) and is also referred to as cassie. It is a winter-flowering shrub, native to the tropical regions of the New World but widely cultivated in the Mediterranean area. The oil has a delightful stimulating bouquet reminiscent of violets. It is highly valued as a component in many fine perfumes.

The beautiful ylang-ylang tree (fig. 16) grows in the East Indies and flowers all the year round, but the best flowers are picked in May and June. The oil of ylang-ylang is obtained by distillation and is one of the more expensive ingredients of quality perfumes with an Oriental note.

A superb oil which is important for perfumery as well as for therapeutic purposes is obtained by distillation from the roots and the heartwood of the sandalwood tree (fig. 17). The tree is indigenous to India but the finest oil is obtained from the raw materials by European firms. With its spicy, stimulating note it is indispensable in scented products for male toiletry such as the famous Windsor soap. In perfume compositions it has the advantage of a slow diffusion rate which makes a fixative unnecessary.

The buds of the clove tree (fig. 18) yield an essential oil which is used in spicy perfume compositions, and in *essence de girofle* (*giroflier* = clove tree). One of the most narcotic of perfumes comes from the hyacinth (Hyacinthus orientalis). It is so overpowering that the plant, like lily of the valley, should never be left in a bedroom or sick-room overnight. Hyacinths are widely cultivated in the South of France but the essential oil is also synthetically produced on a large scale.

No one would pretend that the bouquet of the jonquil or the Pheasant's Eye even vaguely approaches the pleasant. Among all the flowers used in perfumery there is none with a note so reminiscent of excreta and yet it is one of the most interesting scents and, next to the jasmine, the most erogenous. The narcotic effect of these flowers, which play a great part in Greek and Roman mythology (the story of Narcissus), has always been recognized. Both species (N. jonquila and N. poetica) are extensively cultivated in southern France, and the absolute is used mainly in perfumes of the gardenia and *quelques fleurs* complexes.

Even a few grass species play a role in perfumery, notably the Asiatic species Vetiveria zizanioides. The roots of this yield vetiver oil which is playing an increasingly important role in modern perfumery, especially in connection with aldehyde compounds, not only on account of its exhilarating bouquet but also because of its value as a fixative.

The name oak moss is misleading; in fact it is the perfumer's name for several species of lichens, which are non-flowering plants. Out of the 17,000 species extant only a few contain special substances which make them of value in perfumery: the most important are Evernia prunastri (fig. 19), E. mesomorpha, Pseudevernia furfuracea, Lobaria pulmonaria, Ramalia fraxinea, R. farinacea and R. pollinaria. In the trade they are known as *Lichen quercinus viridis*, *Museeus arboreus acaciae et odorante*, *Eichenmoos* (German for oak moss) or *Mousse de chêne*.

Most of these species live epiphytically on trees, usually on the trunk, in relatively humid habitats. Lichens are very sensitive indicators of pollution and are beginning to suffer in industrial parts of the world. The main European supplies come from mountainous regions of Italy (mainly the Piedmont), Herzegovina, Yugoslavia, the Pyrenees and Czechoslovakia where they are collected by local peasants. The perfumer is able to distinguish among the peculiar qualities arising from the geographical location of the plants and also from the habitat, that is, whether they grow on conifers or oak, the latter being considered superior.

The exploitation of oak moss by the perfumer is surrounded by more than the usual secrecy. The main odoriferous ingredients are extracted from the dried material by means of volatile substances. The use of oak moss in perfumery goes back to the 15th century, and during the 17th century and later Ramulina calcavis, another species, was dried and pulverised and used for powdering wigs. A mixture of pulverised lichens, scented with rose-oil, jasmine and ambergris or musk, known as Cyprus powder, was used extensively as a toilet powder in the 17th century. Even more recently lichen powder was used for scenting soap. Islandic Moss (Cetraria islandica) is still used in the preparation of soap as well as cold creams by the cosmetic industry. The perfumer, of course, uses the essential oil of oak moss, the fragrance of which is somewhat similar to musk-lavender, a cheap alternative to ambergris. It is generally used as a harmonizer or as a fixative since it blends well with other essences. For certain perfumes, such as Oriental types or *chypre*, oak moss is a necessity since it is solely responsible for the stimulating erogenous effect ascribed to this composition. It supplies freshness to citron and bergamot and improves the fragrance of rose, jasmine, cassie and neroli. One will also find it in perfumes containing large amounts of ylang-ylang. It is used as a stabilizer with patchouli, musk and vetiver. Even with synthetic oils (amyl and isobutyl salicylate and aceto-phenol) it is a successful partner.

Of the many resins and gums used in perfumery only labdanum should be mentioned. It is obtained by solvent extraction from the resinous leaves of several species of Cistus of the Mediterranean region. The oil, actually an oleoresin, is a valuable fixative, but because of its subtle balsamic fragrance, with a faint similarity to the sweaty odour of a head of hair, it lends a distinctly erotic and stimulating note to the perfume in which it is used. In this respect it is similar in effect to grey ambergris.

The advertisement of a perfume or some other scented product under a flower name does not necessarily mean that the essential oils of the flower in question have been used in its composition. The fragrance of the flower has been created by the perfumer, not necessarily from synthetics, but from other natural products. Examples of perfumes bearing flower names, but which are not made from those flowers, are cyclamen, orchids (with the exception of vanilla), magnolia, freesia, poppy, gardenia, clover (trefoil), lily of the valley and lilac. In some cases a perfume does not even smell much like the flower of its name, which is merely a caprice of its sponsors. The so-called *fougère* type of perfume is one whose name promises a fragrance not in fact possessed by the plant in question. Amongst the thousands of fern species (*fougère* = fern), not one has a fragrance of perfumery value. Perhaps it is the dank mouldiness of some fern habitats in conjunction with the 'green' smell of the actual herb which inspired the perfumer. All *fougère* perfumes are based on lavender-bergamot elements, and the classical type is Houbigant's Fougère Royale.

The fragrance of the essential oil extracted from a plant species is by no means identical with the fragrance of the flower of its origin. The odour which emanates from a living flower is of a complex nature depending on many circumstances, such as the age of the flower, the time of day, the temperature and humidity of the atmosphere. When one stands near a jasmine or rose bush in the open the total aroma analyzed by the sensitive nerve ends within the olfactory membrane of the nasal cavity is composed of scents from all parts of the plant and, not unimportant, even from the soil in which it grows. From experience we know that a rose garden smells quite different on a hot afternoon as opposed to a cool morning, and different again after rain. Thus the extracted fragrance can only represent a fraction of the entire range. If, therefore, a perfumer wants to produce a perfume that smells like rose or violet or lily of the valley at its most characteristic he must recreate it, and in the process he will sometimes have to use ingredients which are not to be found in the chemical make-up of the flower itself.

The essential oil of a plant is an intricate chemical compound and, as mentioned earlier, it can be split up into fractions each of which has its own particular aroma. Odorous substances obtained in this way are referred to as 'isolates'; since they are obtained from natural materials they should not be confused with synthetics, which are produced solely by chemical processes.

When talking about synthetic fragrant substances we must distinguish between two categories, those made in imitation of a known natural fragrance and those which are completely new creations. The extent to which modern chemistry has enriched the perfumer's palette can be demonstrated by the fact that in Eugène Rimmel's time the master perfumer had at his disposal about five hundred different ingredients, whereas today's perfumer has thousands. Most of us wince at the word synthetic, since artificial products are thrust upon us at a frightening rate and in most cases the word denotes a second-rate substitute. This is not necessarily so in the case of perfume. (It must be noted in passing that a number of synthetic materials are even more expensive than the most highly-priced natural substances.)

The increasing affluence of certain societies in all parts of the world has brought in its wake a demand for perfume which can no longer be met by natural resources. The use of perfume, moreover, is no longer the prerogative of the wealthiest classes. In addition there is increased demand for scents from industry, indeed more than ninety per cent of today's perfume production serves an industrial purpose. Advertising agents have discovered that scented merchandise sells better: household cleaning materials, air-fresheners, and even food which, having lost its flavour through mass-production or processing, now requires flavour and aroma to be restored to it. Scented paper, in past centuries reserved solely for love letters, has become commonplace, and sale catalogues emanate the specific scent of the goods they advertise. It has been recorded that an American publisher even went so far as to advertise a new edition of the Scriptures with a prospectus smelling of frankincense. (This feat was no doubt achieved by the modern method called microencapsulation, in which microscopic plastic capsules filled with scent are invisibly attached to book pages.) In this way scent intrudes upon our privacy as the transistor has done, 'blessing' our life with instant music. One has only to look at the various scented sprays on the shelves of the local supermarket, most of them more irritating to a sensitive nose than the odour they are intended to banish, to realize the extent to which industry is making use of odorous materials. The list of uses of synthetic scents could be extended *ad infinitum* but it has no place in a book dealing with containers for the finest perfume. The lover of perfume will perhaps be relieved to know that the scent in the detergent disappearing down the drain in no way owes its existence to the sun of Calabria or Provence but rather to the prosaic surroundings of an industrial plant.

This brief detour, however, is not intended to minimize the important role played by synthetics in the creation of fine perfume, and indeed many of the great names in perfume would be unthinkable without them. Most synthetics are petroleum or coal-tar derivatives, and their history goes back to the year 1834 when the German chemist Mitcherlich achieved a synthesis of nitrobenzene; this later became known as essence of mirbane. (Because of its toxic nature its application is now prohibited.) After the turn of the century there was a veritable explosion in synthetics. It even became possible to duplicate the scent of flowers which had eluded the traditional perfumer, such as the alpine cyclamen, the perfume of which is now recreated by a compound bearing the simple name of paraisopropylalphamethylhydrocinnamic aldehyde. The subtle fragrance of the lily of the valley is similar to the synthetic hydroxy-citronellal, and iso-eugenol is strongly reminiscent of the carnation. Another, known as heliotropin, is far more satisfactory, curiously enough, than the absolute extracted from the heliotrope flower; it is used in the production of inexpensive brands of perfume and for perfuming soap and other cosmetic products.

These are but a few examples of synthetics with a flower-scent connection. There are many others which have not been inspired by nature but devised by man's imagination. The aldehydes and oxyaldehydes group is especially important in perfumery. Aldehydes occur in nature but they are also, to a large extent, created in the chemist's laboratory; their odour can be heavy, narcotic and even suffocating. They are usually found in perfume complexes such as gardenia, *quelques fleurs* and *fougère*, and their faint resemblance to the odour of human sweat lends a subtle erotic note. Typical aldehyde perfumes are Chanel No. 5, L'Interdit and Crêpe de Chine.

I should also mention linalylacetate, a synthetic which can replace the absolute of bergamot if the necessary supply of this otherwise indispensable natural substance is not forthcoming and the enormous demands of *eau de Cologne* makers are not being met. This synthetic is more expensive than the natural oil of bergamot, but there are the advantages of regular availability and a steady price. Another advantage, and this applies to most synthetics, is that it is always of precisely the same composition and quality; unlike the natural product, it is independent of the caprices of nature.

Animal Sources Raw materials from the animal kingdom comprise musk, civet, castoreum and ambergris. These materials are valued either for their own aromatic properties, as in the case of musk, or, more often, as fixatives or stabilizers. Since they evaporate at a very low rate, they tend to equalize the different rates of essential oils contained in a perfume, and thus the fragrant quality of the perfume remains stable long after the bottle has been opened. In their original concentrated forms these animal products have fragrances that can vary from malodorous to directly repugnant; when diluted, the abominable smell is turned into a rather pleasing aroma.

For centuries musk has been valued for its fragrant properties. Its staying power is legendary; Arab mosques built more than a thousand years ago, with mortar containing musk, still emanate its fragrance. Musk was one of the favourite perfumes of the Empress Josephine. She used it lavishly, and it is recorded that many decades after her death the scent of musk still lingered in her apartments at Malmaison. Musk is the most penetrating of all perfumes and its aroma can even be transmitted to metal. Pharmacists used to keep it in a special cabinet, and the scales used for weighing it had to be marked accordingly and not used for other substances. So it is not surprising that musk was never permitted on board ships carrying tea from the East, however well sealed its containers.

Musk is a secretion formed within an abdominal gland near the genital organ of the musk deer (fig. 20), a timid and rather agile animal living in

Fig. 20. Musk deer (Moschus moschiverus)

China, the Northern Himalayas and Tibet at altitudes above 3,000 metres. Each animal yields between 20 and 40 gms. of a bitter substance of a brown to reddish-black colour, and with a pungent smell somewhat reminiscent of faeces. It is usually shipped in dried pods (*musc in vesicis* or *musc en poche*), that is, within the surrounded tissue as removed from the hunted animal, but sometimes it is traded loose (*musc ex vesicis* or *musc en grain*). Neither method guarantees immunity from adulteration: throughout history dealers have tried to falsify this extremely costly product—at the time of writing one ounce costs at least £25—by the admixture of dried blood. Modern chemistry has not yet succeeded in producing a comparable synthetic substance. There are, however, a few substances of a similar note, some synthetic, and some which are secretions of the musk-rat and certain alligators.

Unlike the wild and elusive musk deer, the civet cat (fig. 21) is raised in captivity. It is usually kept on a diet of meat and bananas. Civet, a yellowish-brown substance with a smell resembling that of cat excrement, is produced by a gland situated below the tail in animals of both sexes. Apparently these glands form part of the animal's defence mechanism since the evil-smelling secretion can be squirted at will in the direction of any attacker. This behaviour is exploited by arousing the animal, which then squirts its secretion on to a smooth surface placed near it. Civet can be collected like this or, alternatively, extracted from the cat by means of a spoon. Two subspecies of the civet cat are to be found, one in Asia and the other in North-East Africa. It is the latter, reared in captivity mainly in Ethiopia, the Sudan and parts of Egypt, which supplies the bulk of the civet used in perfumery. Although civet is much less expensive than musk, adulterations are frequently attempted with substances too unsavoury to be mentioned.

When diluted, civet becomes extremely agreeable to the sense of smell and constitutes one of the most powerful and erotically stimulating fragrances in existence. This property is certainly recognized in Tunisia and other parts of North Africa, where civet is used extensively by both sexes and regarded as a most valued bridal gift. In Europe, perfumes with a discernible civet component have always been favoured by the male sex; it was also one of the more common perfumes used for the scenting of gloves during the 16th and 17th centuries. In

Fig. 21. Civet cat (Viverra civetta)

modern perfumery civet is indispensable for certain high-class perfumes, mainly of the *fougère, ambre* and *chypre* types, as well as for all those with a distinctly Oriental note.

The name castoreum stems from the Latin generic name of the animal which yields it, namely the beaver (fig. 22). It is produced in pear-shaped glands situated near the genitalia of both the male and the female. Although the animal was widely distributed throughout Europe during past centuries, it is the Siberian and Canadian beavers which now guarantee a supply. The glands are removed from the dead animal and dried in smoke. The Siberian castoreum, glossy yellowish-brown in colour, is considered superior to the Canadian product which is of a reddish-black appearance. Both appear on the market as extracts, and are rarely traded in their natural state. In post-mediaeval medicine castoreum was used mainly as an antispasmodic drug, but in perfumery it is used for its highly stimulating erotic effect. It is used mostly in perfumes with a leather or tabac base, but also in those of the *ambre* or *chypre* type.

Ambergris is undoubtedly the most enigmatic of all the animal products used in perfumery. Arabian traders made their fortunes with it, over a thousand years ago, and in mediaeval Europe it was prized more highly than gold. Unfortunately there is no space to tell all the legends about this soft fatty substance. It is found drifting on the seas, in pieces ranging in weight from a few grammes to many pounds (the largest single piece on record was about 160 cm. long and almost 75 cm. in diameter). There are two sorts: one is light grey or whitish, emanating a somewhat mouldy smell, and the other dark grey and malodorous. Ambergris is readily soluble in hot alcohol but not in water. We know that it is produced within the intestines of the sperm whale (fig. 23), but are not certain how it is formed. The most plausible theory states that the sharp fins of cuttlefish, which are part of the whale's diet, cause internal irritation and that the tissues react to this by secreting a waxy substance, which is eventually released. We must assume, however, that larger pieces, if not all pieces, come from decomposing carcasses.

The perfumer uses ambergris in an alcoholic solution, which has to be kept for several years before it acquires its characteristic aroma. It is used in high-quality perfumes intended to have a balsamic note. The so-called *ambre*

Fig. 22. Beaver (Castor fiber)

perfumes, although alleged to possess the same erotic effect, have nothing in common with ambergris, despite their name.

If the chemical industry has not yet succeeded in providing perfect substitutes for the other animal products mentioned above, this has been achieved in the case of ambergris. A synthetic substance known as ambropur is as good as the natural product, in the opinion of some experts, and Russian chemists, according to a short note in the *Essential Oil and Perfumery Record*, have obtained a similar substitute from Muscatel sage, known as ambriol.

HOW PERFUME IS CREATED

The task of obtaining basic ingredients for perfumery from raw materials, whether natural or synthetic, belongs to the chemist, the scientist or the technologist. The actual composing of a perfume, involving as many as a hundred ingredients, demands artistic creativity as well as scientific knowledge. A fine perfume is a work of art and a great perfumer is as rare as a great painter or composer. No one has expressed this more clearly than Eugène Rimmel, when he wrote:

> When I say 'the art of the perfumer', let me explain this phrase, which might otherwise appear ambitious. The first musician who tried to echo with a pierced reed the songs of the birds of the forest, the first painter who attempted to delineate on a polished surface the gorgeous scenes which he beheld around him, were both artists endeavouring to copy nature; and so the perfumer, with a limited number of materials at his command, combines them like colours on a palette, and strives to imitate the fragrance of all flowers which are rebellious to his skill, and refuse to yield up their essence. Is he not, then, entitled to claim also the name of an artist, if he approaches even faintly the perfections of his charming models?

Perhaps we should amend this by stating that the number of materials is now great rather than limited, and that the great perfumers of our time do not set out to 'copy nature'—I doubt that this was their predecessors' sole aim—but to use their imagination as well as their talents in the creation of perfumes. A

Pl. IV. *above l. to r*. a. Perfume bottle in the shape of a watch with blue overlay face, gilded numerals, cut perimeter, glass stopper and gilt metal screw-top, French, *c*.1840; b. Venetian scent bottle in the shape of a sea creature made of opaque white glass with coloured glass streaks, attached glass prunts and a tightly fitting silver stopper, *c*.1700; c. shell-shaped amber-coloured glass bottle with opaque white glass threads and pewter screw-top, French (Orléans), *c*.1675. *centre l. to r*. d. Cylindrical overlay bottle, Bohemian, early 19th century; e. scent bottle with opaque white twist and brass screw-top, Italian or Bohemian, early 19th century; f., g. two Bohemian overlay bottles, early 19th century. *below l. to r*. h. Opaline glass smelling or cologne bottle with curved flat cut-out panels, floral ornament and gilding, ground clear glass stopper and hinged hand-tooled silver top, French, 2nd half of 19th century; i. smelling bottle in opaque white glass, decorated with flower and bird motifs, French, 2nd half of 19th century; j. flat oblong scent bottle in opaque white glass, decorated with a young gentleman in a park landscape, German or Bohemian, late 18th/early 19th century. All actual size. *J.M., London*

32

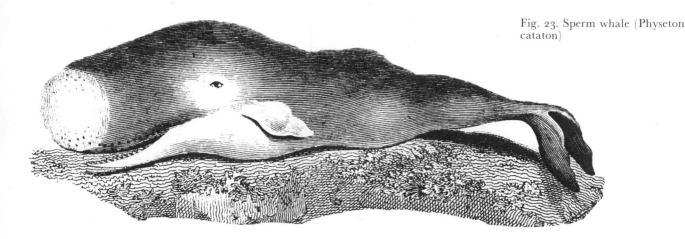

Fig. 23. Sperm whale (Physeton cataton)

perfume, however constituted, is always the result of thought and reflection.[2] Modern technology has introduced methods which permit the analysis of essential oils, such as gas-liquid chromatography, infra-red and ultra-violet spectroscopy, mass spectroscopy, and chemical apparatus which can separate fragrant substances for analysis, such as optical rotary dispersion; but in the end it is the time-honoured art of the perfumer, or '*grand nez*' as he is called in France, which makes a new perfume. He must have an extraordinary olfactory sense and be endowed with a retentive memory for scent; he must be able to tell whether an absolute of, let us say, jasmine comes from India, Provence or Spain and, more important, he must be able to identify by smell the ingredients of a given perfume and estimate the proportion of each.

What makes his task especially difficult, and in this respect it differs from the comparable task of the wine-maker, is the continued diffusion of his material. As described earlier, every perfume, like every essential oil, goes through various phases or 'notes', and the fixative chosen to govern the end note must be very delicately balanced against the other ingredients. The perfumer's aim in this is to ensure that the quality of the perfume in the bottle continues once the seal is broken, and also that the perfume on the skin retains its characteristic aroma; to achieve this, not one of the components should evaporate at a faster rate than the others. The durability of a perfume in the bottle is referred to as its life cycle, meaning the time from when the bottle is first opened until the last drop has been used. A good perfume should retain its quality for a long time, but it is nevertheless wise to buy high-quality perfume in the smallest possible quantity.

Only a few perfumes have been created by accident. Usually the making of a perfume starts with an idea, which is often dictated by the fashion of the time. Thus a perfume can be commissioned like a piece of music, but it may take many years before the final composition reaches the market.

The term 'note' in connection with perfumery is by no means arbitrary: on the contrary, it has been deliberately borrowed from the world of music. It is quite amusing to learn that a writer on perfume who was himself a perfumer, Septimus Piesse, invented a system by which he could arrange scents into harmonies; each one was given a note from a tonal scale spanning six and a half octaves, so that the note A was for lavender, B for mint, C for pineapple, and so on.

Everyday experience shows the difficulty of describing a smell in words. It is no wonder that throughout history perfumers have endeavoured to work out a classification of fragrances, though they have never arrived at a satisfactory one. Strictly speaking there is no such thing as a measurable pure smell. Nevertheless, the perfumer speaks of perfumes with a spicy note, a woody note, a leathery note, an Oriental note and so on.

The perfumer's traditional working place is a u-shaped laboratory table,

Pl. V. *left* Two mould-blown scent bottles decorated in high relief with a coat of arms; pewter screw-tops. French (Orléans), *c.*1680, perhaps made for the Flemish market, 100 mm high. *right* Two blown gourd-shaped phials with the interior surface silvered; pewter screw-tops. French (Orléans), late 17th/early 18th century. 60 mm and 80 mm high. *DROM-Schatzkammer*

Pl. VI. *left* Atomizer, clear cut-glass flashed with red, silver-gilt mounts. Bohemian, 3rd quarter of 19th century. 145 mm high. *centre l.* Perfume bottle in ruby red glass, with silver-gilt mounts and stopper. German, late 17th/early 18th century. 70 mm high. *centre r.* Cologne bottle for the dressing table. Clear glass, panels flashed with red and with wheel-engraved diaper and foliate motifs; silver mount and stopper. Bohemian, mid-19th century. 170 mm high. *right* Perfume bottle of cut overlay glass (clear glass on red). German, late 19th century. 105 mm high. *DROM-Schatzkammer*

with ranks of small shelves around it carrying most of the ingredients for his task. This is known as the organ (*les orgues*), because of the resemblance to an organ console. (Modern perfumers, however, find this arrangement impracticable and have, in most cases, abandoned it in favour of a laboratory bench.) His main tools are strips of absorbent testing paper, the so-called *mouillettes*, which he dips into various bottles and then allows to dry. They are fixed to his desk with metal clips, so that they are readily accessible, and kept for days and sometimes weeks. By regular sniffing he is able to gauge the changes undergone by a substance during a period of time. Patiently he builds up the base of his perfume using the array of liquid ingredients as a painter uses the colours on his palette, and always recording the quantities used. But this art of blending a perfume cannot be exercised without reference to other factors, such as the time of day, the season, conditions in the country to which the product will be exported and, of course, the nature of the intended market—perfumes for the teenage market will naturally be very different from those suited to ladies of advanced years. Finally, before it can go into production, the perfume must be tested for skin tolerance. (This is, of course, only a cursory description of the entire process; if given in detail it would fill the pages of this book from cover to cover.)

Perhaps the true connoisseur of fine perfume is as rare as the connoisseur of art or music. In the past there were the great dealer-perfumers, men like René, Houbigant, Charles Lilly, Piver, Millot, Guerlain, Rimmel, Luby, Chardin, Coty, Molinard and others, who were perfumers in their own right. After Houbigant, Pierre-François Pascal Guerlain was the first of the modern perfumers, and also one of the greatest and most admired of the '*grands nez*'. His house, founded over a century ago, has produced five generations of notable perfumers, the foremost among them being Jacques Guerlain. Of his forty-three perfumes a few, such as Shalimar and Mitsouko, have become classics. But today's great perfumers remain anonymous and sell their creations to the big names of *haute couture* (the '*assimiles*' as they are called by the traditional professional perfumer) such as Chanel, Dior, Rochas and others. To the present day the great perfumers, like great chefs, have been male, but Bandit, a well-known perfume from the house of Piquet, was composed by Mademoiselle Cellier, and two very successful perfumes, Cassandra and Antilope, are the creations of Jacqueline Fraysse, daughter of a famous family of perfumers.

A newly-created perfume will be made available in a variety of forms. As a perfume in the strict sense it will consist of twelve to twenty per cent of a perfume compound contained in alcohol, and a trace of distilled water. The misleading term *extrait* was frequently used in the past to describe this strength of perfume, and more recently it has been inappropriately named 'handkerchief perfume'. Less concentrated perfumes, containing eight to ten per cent of a perfume compound, are sometimes referred to as *eau de parfum* or *eau de senteur*. Both types are liable to deterioration when exposed to air and intense light and must therefore be kept in small bottles with tight-fitting stoppers.

Eau de toilette (also known as toilet water) and *eau de Cologne* are terms for preparations which contain, respectively, five to eight per cent and two to four per cent of essential oils dissolved in aqueous alcohol. The two names are often used interchangeably. An *eau de toilette* is characterized by one dominant fragrance (e.g. lavender water), while *eau de Cologne*, discussed in some detail below, contains as basic ingredients the oils of verbena, bergamot, citron, neroli and orange, and of lavender and rosemary as well. Both are purchased in larger quantities than perfume and usually they are contained in large bottles for use at the dressing table, but sometimes in smaller bottles to be carried on the person.

I mention cream perfume only for the sake of completeness, and likewise the recently-developed solid perfumes with five to ten per cent of a perfume compound in a cream or wax base. Both types have important cosmetic applications.

THE STORY OF *EAU DE COLOGNE*

Although the city of Cologne, always a focal point of European culture, has given its name to these widely used toilet waters, in fact it is hard to determine the actual place of origin. One assumes that they were first compounded in Italian monasteries, since the main ingredients are the essential oils of citrus fruit. There is also a distinct possibility that they were made in other Mediterranean countries as well, especially Spain and Portugal.

Some sources maintain that the formula was brought from Milan to Cologne by Paul de Feminis around 1690. This may be true, but it is generally accepted that the first cologne produced there on a commercial scale was that of Johann Maria Farina (1685–1766) (fig. 24). The Rhinelands have throughout the centuries been a melting pot for people of different languages and cultures. During the 17th and 18th centuries it attracted numerous Italian immigrants, two of the most successful of them being the brothers Farina from Santa Maria Maggiore near Dome d'Ossola. The elder, Johann Baptist, established himself in Cologne in 1709 and was later joined by his brother Johann Maria. He started a *Kommissions- und Speditionshandel* (a kind of retail and import trade) and also a shop selling *Galanteriewaren* (all varieties of fancy goods). But it was the

Fig. 24. Johann Maria Farina (1685–1766). *Farina Gegenüber, Cologne*

35

younger brother who introduced the production of *aqua mirabilis*, as it was then called, into the business. It was only after the death of Johann Baptist in 1732 that the product, made according to a secret formula, increased in popularity, and was produced and traded in large quantities. It was used, however, in a manner entirely different from that of the present day, on account of its supposed medicinal properties, (to which the names *aqua mirabilis*, *eau admirable* or *Wunderwasser* refer). It is hard to imagine people of the day taking it 'once or twice a week in a dose of fifty to sixty drops in wine, water, warm broth, or other liquids as a remedy against stomach upsets, headaches, toothache, unrequited love, labour pains, halitosis, strokes or even as a prophylactic against the plague', but indeed they did. Each bottle was equipped with a *Wasserzettel*, rather as the Continental mineral waters are today, namely a label describing the *Würkung und Tugenden*, the vouched-for good effects and properties of the liquid (see fig. 25). Many of these properties may be queried, but the antiseptic action of this elixir is undeniable, and when applied externally cologne will certainly alleviate the pain caused by inflammation of the skin, cuts and bruises. There is still a famous firm in Cologne, in fact, which manufactures a well-known folk remedy known as *Klosterfrau-Melissengeist* for complaints similar to those listed by Farina. This product is based mainly on the essential oil of balm (Melissa officinalis), and is similar in composition and effect to the famous *eau des Carmes* still produced in French convents and monasteries. Whether such preparations influence the health of the individual I leave the reader to ponder; the cynic will no doubt point out that most ailments are self-healing anyway.

By the early 19th century the medicinal pretentions of *eau admirable* were fading into obscurity. Napoleon had proclaimed in 1810 that the formula of all medicaments must be made public, and if the makers of *eau de Cologne* had

Fig. 25. *Rosolen* flask, one of the earliest commercial bottles for the sale of *eau de Cologne*. Behind, a printed pamphlet describing the medicinal properties of its contents. German, 17th century. *Farina Gegenüber, Cologne*

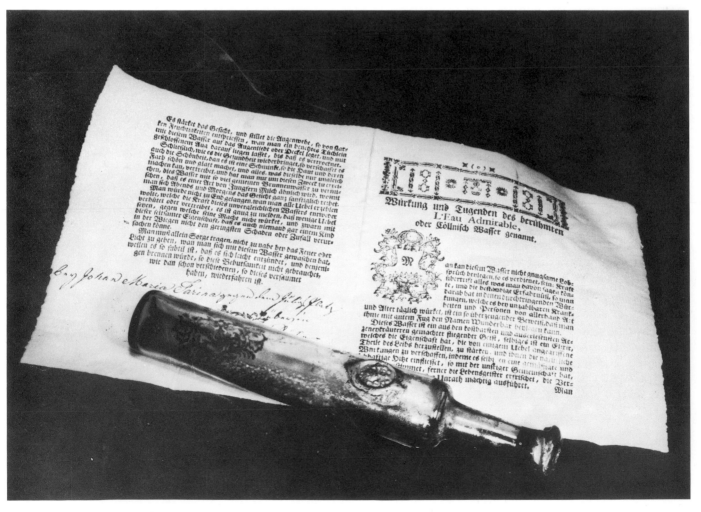

continued to market their product as a medicine, they would have had to reveal their closely guarded secret. Competition was increasing, and therefore they ceased to advertise the medicinal properties of cologne and stressed its powers as a freshener, for which it is still valued today.

According to most sources, the name *eau de Cologne* was first used by officers of the French army involved in the Seven Years' War (1756–63), who learned to appreciate this toilet water during their passage through Cologne. But in the archives of the House of Farina there is a letter in Farina's own hand, dated 1742, in which he himself uses the term *eau de Cologne* for the first time. The German translation *Kölnisch Wasser*, applied to a product made by an Italian and given a French name, did not come into use until twenty-five years later.

Johann Maria Farina's success as a businessman—and he was first and foremost a businessman who knew how to promote his product, rather than a perfumer—is unprecedented in the history of perfumery. A life-long bachelor, he died a wealthy man in 1766, and the business passed to his nephew, also named Johann Maria. Naturally, so successful an enterprise could not long remain without competitors. Farina's rivals were not content with imitating his *eau de Cologne*, they even used his name. Some went so far as to hire partners with the name of Farina, even though they were no relation of the founders of the firm (the name, meaning flour, is common in Italy). J. M. Farina had given his firm the name *Farina gegen dem Jülichplatz über in Cöln*, which later became *Gegenüber dem Jülichplatz*, meaning 'Farina opposite the Jülich Square'. Over the years there were no less than a hundred and fourteen instances of rivals using his name, in conjunction with the '*gegenüber dem*' motto, until the original name was finally secured towards the end of the last century by an appeal to law. The tale makes interesting reading, and it gives a fascinating picture of trade malpractices and early industrial espionage over a period of two centuries. The legal haggling evoked interest even beyond the borders of Germany. Numerous cartoons appeared in French journals poking fun at the affair, and in the Parisian *Charivari* the satirist Maon wrote:

> Et chaque jour le Rhin vers Cologne charrie
> De nombreux Farinas, tout seuls, tous Jean Marie.

Dubochereau, Napoleon's perfume supplier, fought an endless war against Farina for the honour of being known as '*Distillateur de l'Empresse Josephine*'. But his efforts to oust Farina as supplier to the crowned heads of France were quite unsuccessful, as evidenced by a label on a *Rosolen* flask of about 1835. It reads: *Eau de Cologne de Jean Marie Farina, le plus ancien distillateur de la plus véritable Eau de Cologne. Fournisseur Breveté de S. M. Louis Philippe, Roi des Français, S. M. Marie-Amélie, Reine des Français. S. A. R. Monseigner Ferdinand Philippe d'Orléans, Prince Royal des Français, S. M. Guillaume IV, Roi d'Angleterre, S. M. Adelaide, Reine d'Angleterre.* The quarrels and the publicity they caused had a beneficial effect on the sales of the product, and during the first half of the 19th century *eau de Cologne* was used lavishly throughout Europe.

The most prominent among Farina's serious rivals was a firm which still exists and which is known throughout the world by a number: *4711*. This enterprise was founded in Cologne in 1792 by the banker Ferdinand Mühlens who, it is said, received his recipe for *aqua mirabilis* from a Carthusian monk as recognition of hospitality extended to the latter during wartime difficulties. The origin of the number *4711* as the firm's trademark—and a modern advertising agency could hardly have done better—is quite amusing: the French revolutionary armies began to occupy Cologne in 1794, and it was found, to their commander's annoyance, that the houses in that quaint old German city were not numbered. In order to find their way around, which was important since the troops were billeted all over the place, the French introduced compulsory house numbers. Ferdinand Mühlens' residence in the

Fig. 26. *Rosolen* flask with original label, in green glass. German, late 19th century. 213 mm high. *Kunstgewerbemuseum, Cologne*

Fig. 27. Metal *eau de Cologne* bottle, given to travellers as a souvenir. German, early 20th century. 70 mm high. *J. M., London*

Glockengasse was given the number *4711*.

The products of both Farina Gegenüber and *4711* are still made in Cologne and have remained unchanged. They are the classic *eaux de Cologne*. Farina's cologne is of the subtle, sweetish neroli type, and the more widely distributed *4711* has the somewhat penetrating character of the bergamot type.

The vogue for *eau de Cologne* during the 19th century stimulated perfumers outside Germany to create their own; the house of Lubin, for example, produced its Eau de Lubin which it advertised as being especially suitable for gentlemen attending the races, and in 1860 Guerlain composed his Eau de Cologne Impériale expressly for the Empress Eugénie. Of today's varieties only a few can be mentioned here: the Brazilian Queen Mercedes' *eau de Cologne* which, on account of its ether content, has a slightly euphoric-narcotic effect; the Russian *eau de Cologne*, also known as Russian Leather and characterized by the aroma of birch-tar oil; and finally *eau de Portugal* and *Florida Water*, all of which are nothing but variations of the same theme.

Since *eau de Cologne* was originally retailed as a medicine it is not surprising that early cologne flasks resemble the medicine bottles of the period. The phials which Farina chose for his *aqua mirabilis*, the so-called *Rosolenflaschen*, were long cylindrical flasks with a drawn-out neck upon a narrow flat shoulder. The base was either flat, displaying a coarse pontil mark, or slightly kicked (fig. 26). This shape can be traced back to ancient bottles of the 15th and 16th centuries. There are a few 15th-century flasks of a similar shape in the Kunstgewerbe-museum in Cologne which, besides being of darker metal, differ from the *Rosolen* of the late 17th and early 18th centuries by having a much shorter neck and a broad flattened rim; in some specimens the neck is reduced to a mere constriction and the diameter above it exceeds the diameter of the body of the bottle. Almost all bottles of this kind are in the typical colours of German *Waldglas*. This term (*Wald* = wood, forest) applies to a wide range of primitive glass produced in central European glass-houses from the 15th century onwards. These glass-houses were usually established in wooded areas of the Mittlege-birge mountain range because of the abundance of wood available as fuel. The colours of the glass, usually green or bluish-green but sometimes brown, were not deliberately intended but caused by the iron content of the sand used in its making; the other main ingredient, potash, was obtained from beechwood ash.

Rosolen bottles were used for *eau de Cologne* up to the end of the 19th century. The last of them were, of course, machine-made, and these are often of a slightly conical shape and, sometimes, elliptical in cross-section. This type of bottle is often unearthed from Victorian rubbish tips by the modern bottle collector. Early *eau de Cologne* flasks, the length of which can vary from 17 to 22 cm., display a marked irregularity: it was virtually impossible to produce blown bottles of even shape at an economical price. In order to comply with the law the *eau de Cologne* was measured in a graded metal jug before being poured into the flasks, which were then corked and closed with tape and sealing wax. Eighteenth-century *Rosolen*, complete with sealed label and cork stopper, are relatively rare. Early bottles are marked with Farina's coat of arms embossed in sealing wax (fig. 25), but later printed labels were used.

Present-day manufacturers, both in Germany and in France, have adopted these pleasing antique shapes for their bottles, but even the inexperienced collector will not mistake them for their ancestors. From 1830 onwards the firm of Farina gradually replaced the *Rosolen* with the stocky, shouldered Molanus bottle named after the distiller Nikolaus Molanus. This shape facilitated marketing and could be produced more cheaply by mechanical means. To the collector of fine glass this bottle is of no interest but it may excite the ardent bottle digger.

Chapter 2
Solid Perfume Containers

THE POMANDER

The pomander, in Western civilization, is the oldest portable container for holding solid aromatic substances. Its history can be traced back to the 12th century when, in 1174, Emperor Frederick Barbarossa is known to have received several pomanders in the form of golden apples filled with musk as a gift from King Baldwin of Jerusalem. The description of these metallic fruits reveals the extent of the goldsmith's achievements at this early date, and we can safely assume, moreover, that similar pomanders were in use in Europe during the preceding centuries. This assumption is supported by the survival of an apple-shaped golden pin-head of the 6th century, 30 mm. in diameter, and filled with resinous substances, which was found in a prince's tomb at Wittlislingen, and is now to be seen in the Bayerisches Nationalmuseum. Most pomanders dating from the 12th to the 16th century are apple- or globe-shaped, made of gold or silver and not infrequently studded with gem stones or pearls. The container, after all, had to be worthy of its extremely costly contents, namely musk or a mixture of musk and other aromatic substances such as civet, castoreum, tragacanth (a resinous vegetable substance) and pulverised spices kneaded into a ball.

The earliest examples are known under the German names *Bisamapfel* (*Bisam* = musk, *Apfel* = apple), *Bisamknopf* (*Knopf* = button) or *Riechapfel* (*riechen* = to smell), or by the French terms *pomme de musc* or *pomme de senteur*. In Latin inventories they are referred to as *pomum pro odore*. Whatever the shape of the vessel, it was always pierced to allow the perfume to disperse. On the basic principle of a pierced container mediaeval craftsmen created a multitude of tiny works of art, many of which can be seen in our museums. Their oriental origins are indicated by the fact that Frederick Barbarossa's gift came from the King of Jerusalem, and also by the mediaeval references to pomanders '*à la façon de Damaz*'. The earliest descriptions are to be found in French treasure inventories, where pomanders are also mentioned as Granate apples (*en façon de Grenade*). The same sources reveal that besides the vessels filled with musk other pieces, such as rosary beads, pendants or devotional figures, were coated with a musk-based paste.

The existence of pomanders is also recorded in contemporary paintings; for instance, a rather larger specimen *en façon de Grenade*, most probably reserved for royalty, is seen in Hans Baldung's 'Adoration' in the former Kaiser Friedrich Museum, Berlin. A typical *Bisamapfel* can be observed in a painting forming part of the Hersbruck Altar in the Germanisches Nationalmuseum, Nuremberg, and in a most enchanting painting of a Hapsburg prince by Hans Miedlich (1515–73) in the Kunsthistorisches Museum, Vienna, a *Bisamapfel* is worn suspended from the girdle of the child (fig. 28). Another early representation, this time showing a pomander worn as a necklace, is to be seen in the fresco 'Testament of Moses' by Luca Signorelli (*c.* 1445–1523) in Orvieto Cathedral. In a painting of a gentleman dating from *c.* 1543 by Lucas Cranach in the Württembergische Staatsgalerie, Stuttgart, we see a small *Bisamapfel* hanging on a golden chain beneath a jewelled medallion. Similar specimens can be seen in a painting by Martin Schaffner in Ulm Cathedral, in a portrait of a gentleman by Bartholomäus Bruyn the Elder (*c.* 1550) in Rohonez Castle and in another portrait of a gentleman by Christoph Amberger in Lübeck.

In many instances there is disagreement among experts concerning the identification of objects in paintings, but I would tentatively suggest that a pomander is also to be seen in a painting by Jan Gossart, 'The Adoration of the Kings', *c.* 1505 (National Gallery, London), worn by the turbaned figure on the left, and that it is a pomander rather than a rattle suspended on the long, highly ornate chain worn by a daughter of Roberto Strozzi in the delightful portrait by Titian (*c.* 1477–1576) (Staatliche Museen, Berlin). A thorough iconography of the pomander would list at least two dozen other paintings or engravings in which pomanders could be identified.

Fig. 28. Painting of a Hapsburg Prince by Hans Mielich (1515–1573), showing a pomander suspended from the girdle, together with other magic objects.
Kunsthistorisches Museum, Vienna

40

Most pomanders are of the pierced globular type, either suspended on a chain or, as a smaller version, attached to a finger ring. From their frequent representation in paintings as well as repeated reference to them in domestic and ecclesiastical inventories, one gains an impression of their importance to the élite of the day. It is reported that Archduke Siegmund of the Tyrol purchased no less than twenty-seven on one occasion alone, in 1487.

With the approach of the 17th century musk was gradually being replaced; it continued to be scarce, and its cost rose with the increase in demand. Its place was taken by other aromatic substances, chiefly ambergris, though this too was expensive. It was ambergris which gave the pomander its name, 'pomander' being a contraction of *pomme* and *ambre* (from the French *ambre gris* or *ambre blanc*). The term *pomme d'ambre* is also found. Although the name signifies a shape similar to that of an apple—and the object did indeed for a long time conform to that shape—it later assumed many guises according to the fantasy of the craftsman and his patron, and the spirit of the times. The ultimate forms were those of the spice box and smelling flask, but the dividing lines between these and the pomander are often blurred. The change, however, did not coincide with the introduction of ambergris. Already in the 16th century there were pomanders in the shape of pears, pine cones and the very popular heart-shape. The Archduchess Anna of Austria owned one 'like an Agnus Dei', and in 1547 she bequeathed to her husband a golden pomander decorated with a portrait of him and herself. Other crowned heads, the Emperor Charles V for instance, owned heart-shaped pomanders. One interesting heart-shaped piece, probably made by Friesian craftsmen, was found in the tomb of Count Anton I of Oldenburg (1505–73) in the Church of St. Lamberti in Oldenburg. The front of this silver-gilt capsule bears a Christ monogram superimposed on an anchor and the inscription *in hoc signo vinces* (in this sign you will conquer). The reverse is elegantly pierced. (It is now in the Oldenburg Museum, and a similar piece is in the Victoria and Albert Museum.)

At some European courts more original shapes were in use: in the Kunsthistorisches Museum, Vienna, there is one in the form of a musk-coated golden bear set with diamonds, rubies and pearls, and the Schatzkammer of the Residenz in Munich has a similar vessel which can also serve as a beaker; the bear's head is removed to reveal a small scent container in the neck. These adults' toys, exhibiting typically Mannerist designs, were made in Augsburg around 1575. In the same collection there are some pierced wooden boxes made for ambergris; this type would have been used mainly during the 16th and 17th centuries. The Oldenburg Museum has among its treasures an ambergris heart enclosed in gold filigree work, and a fine gold-mounted piece of ambergris is on show in the jewellery gallery of the Victoria and Albert Museum. The price of ambergris, it should be noted, was far in excess of that of gold, and a rosary with beads of solid ambergris, now in the Munich Schatzkammer and listed in the inventory for 1635 (although its date is probably earlier) was once no doubt a most treasured possession.

The British Museum (Franks Bequest) boasts a 16th-century open sphere, intended for a musk-ball, constructed in thin gold with applied wire-work and studded with pearls. There is also a 16th-century Spanish 'perfume-ball' set with emeralds. And in the Kriss Collection (Bayerisches Nationalmuseum, Munich), there is a rosary with a miniature pomander and other devotional items inserted between the red coral beads.

One of the strangest varieties to be found is the locket-type pomander illustrated in fig. 29, in which one side simulates the face of a woman in her prime while the other grimly represents the grinning features of a skull. The skull-shaped pomander was fairly common in countries north of the Alps during the 15th and 16th centuries; there is a superb specimen in the form of a complete skull, with a snake curling behind the suspensory loop, in a private

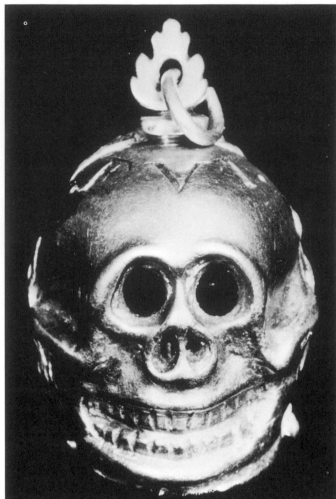

Fig. 29. Janiform pomander, silver-gilt, one side showing a woman's face and inscribed *Sum* (I am), the other side showing a skull-face and inscribed *Fui* (I have been). French or German, 16th century. 30 mm high. *DROM-Schatzkammer*

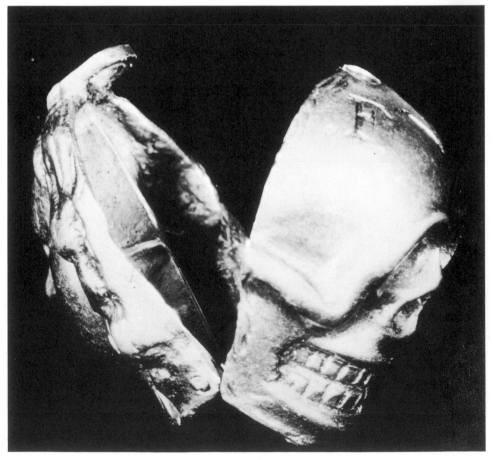

collection in Munich. In an article on pomanders[3] Edward Wenham records a golden skull enamelled in ivory colours so that at first glance it is readily taken to be made of ivory. I was unable to trace the whereabouts of this interesting specimen. Wenham also includes, and illustrates, a piece from an Edinburgh collection which seems to me the most remarkable in this category: it is a realistically-shaped silver apple with a stalk and two leaves, but bearing the impression of a bite effected by five upper and five lower teeth and, on the opposite side, the inscription 'A.D. 1628 From Man Came Woman—From Woman Came Sin—From Sin Came Death'. Wenham suggests that the inscription was added by an embittered misanthrope who interpreted the teethmarks 'as Eve's bite, and having removed the movable section of the silver apple and finding a death's-head inside, extended his apothegm to include death.' I am tempted to suggest that the inscription might have been the wry comment of a gentleman who knew the effects of syphilis. The exquisitely modelled pomander-skull contained within the apple is of particular interest since the interior of the lower jaw holds a miniature with the Resurrection as its theme.

The object in fig. 30 is reminiscent of the pomander-shape—this was certainly the maker's intention. On a silvergilt dish of a pleasing undulating shape stands what is in fact a bag of sweet-smelling substances in a loosely woven reddish material, fringed above and below in yellow. The bag, however, is intended to look like the voluminous skirt of a burgher's wife, and the bust of the lady herself, wrought in silver, is attached to the top of it at the point where the farthingale would have been worn. (This stiffened under-garment was worn around the hips to achieve the desired fashionable shape of the period, and may possibly have contained aromatic substances of some kind). The marriage of

Fig. 30. Pomander-shaped sachet on a silver-gilt dish and surmounted by a silver-gilt figure of a burgher's wife. German (Caspar Wendl of Munich), c.1625. 60 mm high. *DROM-Schatzkammer*

the two materials, metal and cloth, is harmoniously achieved by the repetition of a motif: the curling fringe-like ornamentation in the metal echos the fringe of the skirt or bag. This object, which functions as a pomander on account of the loose weave of the material, forms an interesting link between the pomander and the sachet. Throughout the centuries powdered or crushed herbs have been put into silk or linen bags, or ornamented envelopes, and the sachet has then been placed in a drawer or hung up in a wardrobe to impart the scent to bed-linen or clothes.

Most of the early pomanders were not divided, being designed to hold a single piece of solid perfume, but there are a few examples with divisions into two or three chambers. The later segmented pomander solved the problem of storing several aromatic substances within one container. Usually they were based on the traditional apple shape. They were most sophisticated gadgets and also pieces of outstanding beauty, occupying a prominent place in late mediaeval and Renaissance jewellery. The inventor of the first of them must have been inspired by an orange when he arranged the individual loculi around a central column. The segments, ranging from four to eight in number, are hinged to the column at its base, and in the closed position they are held together by a lid, shaped variously as a bell, a bowl or a saucer, which screws into the central column and bears the suspensory loop. Each of the loculi is closed by a sliding lid on its ventral side, and usually the name of the substance contained within is engraved on the lid. (Segmented pomanders with open loculi are relatively rare.) This type of pomander was in favour for almost two centuries and naturally there were many variations on the theme. In many specimens the central column, round or angular, is hollow, housing yet another compartment. As a rule the pomander rests on a domed foot; in some examples this is itself another lidded compartment, and in others the base may act as a seal or as a unguent spreader. In extremely rare cases, all dating from the 17th century, the bottom of the foot consists of a beautifully chiselled, perforated plate behind which pieces of sponge drenched with aromatic liquids were placed; this classifies the hollow foot as an early vinaigrette.

The oldest known segmented pomander—and in my opinion the most beautiful—is in the Bayerisches Nationalmuseum, Munich, and was made around 1470 by a Rhenish silversmith (fig. 31). It is about 40 mm. high and, deviating from the usual shape, it is made in the form of a walnut. German inventories list this type as *Betnuss* (*beten* = to pray, *Nuss* = nut). The outer

Fig. 31. *Betnuss*, silver segmented pomander in the shape of a walnut. German (Rhenish), 15th century. 40 mm high. *Bayerisches National-museum, Munich*

Fig. 32. Segmented pomander in silver, richly engraved and suspended from a chain: *left* opened, showing hunting scenes engraved on loculi; lids engraved with the names of contents (Zibet, Ambra, Bisam, Zitronia BA, Rosmarin B, Angelia BA), *right* closed. South German, late 16th century (the chain is not contemporary). 65 mm high. *DROM-Schatzkammer*

surface is decorated with chased text-bearing ribbons, the resulting pattern recalling the natural convolutions of the walnut shell. The main difference between this and most other known segmented pomanders lies in the fact that here the shell is also pierced: thus we have a true pomander in the traditional sense, whereas later pieces may be considered mainly as storage containers on account of their completely closed loculi. The lateral surfaces of each of the four sections of this piece, as well as the surface of the central column, are beautifully embossed with figures of saints in the style of the great German sculptors of the period.

A later German example is illustrated in fig. 32; here the loculi are richly engraved with hunting scenes. Extraordinarily fine pomanders were also made by French and Italian craftsmen during the 17th century. A superb sexagonal segmented pomander in silver-gilt, enamelled with formal floral motifs and set with gems, is illustrated in pl. I.

We must assume that pomanders of this type came to England, as did most artistic and cultural inspirations, via France. The earliest known English examples were produced during the last two decades of the 16th century, and were gradually replaced by the spice box and, finally, by the vinaigrette.

The so-called Royal Portrait pomanders are remarkable: they are of the sexagonal type, with the dorsal surface of each segment bearing an engraved portrait of an English monarch (Henry IV, Edward IV, Henry VII, Henry VIII and Elizabeth I.) They date from the first quarter of the 17th century. The execution of the engraving is not always to the standard of contemporary English work, and certainly they cannot be compared with the exquisitely finished continental pieces of the same period. Whereas most segmented pomanders follow the original globe-shape more or less, occasionally one finds specimens shaped like pears or even gourds. There must have been a short-lived revival for the pomander in the Victorian era: a few examples are known, their loculi set with turquoises, and made in 1867 by Robert Thornton, London.[4]

One of the most extravagant of the segmented pomanders (illustrated by Wenham) has three scroll feet and is placed on a highly ornate silver tripod, of which the feet are shaped like pomegranates.

A much less complicated and certainly less expensive device is the lantern-shaped or cruciform pomander (see fig. 33) which evolved after the middle of

Fig. 33. Cruciform pomander, the handle containing a perfume spray; silver. English, 17th century. 120 mm high. *Wella Museum, Darmstadt*

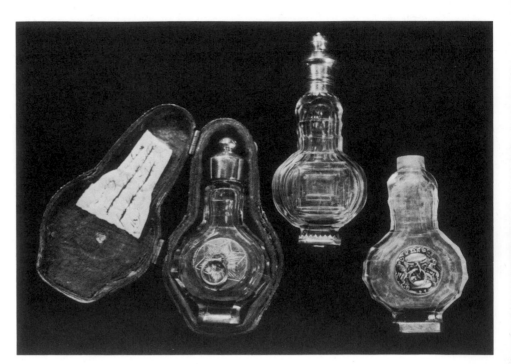

Fig. 34. Smelling bottles with a
small pomander on top of a hinged
silver cap; *left* original case with
written dedication dated 1691.
English, late 17th to early 18th
century. 80 mm high (*right*).
Dr. Spiers (*left*) *and J. M., London*
(*centre and right*)

the 17th century. It cannot have been very popular, judging by the small number which can be traced today. The illustration is almost self-explanatory: the four compartments are each closed by a screwed lid and the only reminder of the original pomander shape is the perforated screwed-on finial which is spherical. Some examples contained a spray beneath the finial for the dispersal of liquid perfume. Whereas most cruciform containers were suspended from a chain or string, the one in the illustration is unusual, in that it was designed to be carried by hand.

A rather more complex specimen, mid-18th-century in origin, I think, was in a collection at Cardiff.[5] It consists of a cylindrical stem, containing six separate loculi, with one end terminating in a spherical, pierced pomander and the other in a whistle. It is certainly an unusual combination, In the same collection there is an example of a further development: the stem, tapering into a flat foot, bears an urn-shaped container for musk and this is topped by a screwed-on thimble covering a bobbin for silk. The tapering stem serves as a needle-case and the foot as a seal.

I was unable to trace the origin of these pomanders but am inclined to regard them as English. In comparing the pomander finial with the silver mounts of two of the glass smelling bottles illustrated in fig. 34, one notices a similarity in style and finish which can hardly be accidental. The finials on these glass bottles were undoubtedly intended as pomanders, but their size reflects the diminished importance of these objects. It is intriguing to see how, in both examples, the pomander has been incorporated in a single bottle with two items which superseded it, the smelling box and the smelling flask.

THE SMELLING BOX

The smelling box did not suddenly displace the pomander—both existed side by side throughout the 16th century—but it became increasingly popular during the 17th and entirely usurped the place of the pomander in the late 18th century. This development is related, of course, to the changing pattern of the application of perfume. But objects of this nature cannot be placed in rigid categories. Whereas the pomander is usually regarded as a pierced vessel, allowing for the dissipation of its contents, a box is by definition a closed container intended for storage. Yet boxes in a variety of shapes have been used in either capacity. The earliest known example, a pendant book-shaped silver

capsule with a Maltese cross embossed in the lid, came to light in a woman's
tomb dating from the 6th century in Szentes-Nagyhegy, eastern Hungary
(Kriss Collection). A most remarkable Renaissance pomander is illustrated in
an article by Hugh Tait:[6] it is in the form of a book about 50 mm. high. The
openwork tracery of the front and back 'covers', executed in a typical Mannerist
strapwork pattern, is enamelled in black, white and blue, and each corner of
the book, set with a table-cut diamond, is opened by sliding out a panel at the
bottom. This beautiful piece is probably English. An English-made box of the
early 17th century, now in the Wellcome Medical Historical Museum,[7] is
another example of the book shape; the spine is engraved with a diaper
pattern, and at each end of the book there are three divisions for aromatic
substances.

Among the many animal-shaped smelling boxes the fish (fig. 35) features
prominently—the shape was also frequently used for bottles from the 17th to
the 20th centuries. The snail-shaped smelling container in fig. 36 is rare, but an
almost identical pomander (with one side of the shell in openwork) is to be
seen in the Kriss Collection, and another fine piece is in the Victoria and Albert
Museum.

During the second half of the 18th century numerous smelling boxes were
still produced and used side by side with the scent bottle. The shape of the étui
was usually adopted for these late pieces, and their decorative style was
typically rococo, as in fig. 37. The early part of the 19th century witnessed a
last revival of this type of container, which was often made in imitation of 16th-
and 17th-century bottles. The Museum für Kunst und Gewerbe, Hamburg,
holds several silver pieces shaped like animals, of which one of the most
remarkable is one in the form of a seated heraldic lion. Among the others in the
collection one takes the form of an acorn pendant, and another is in the
restrained shape of a neo-classical urn. Many of these late boxes did not actually
hold solid perfume but were filled with pieces of sponge or even cotton wool
drenched with liquid perfume. In this respect they illustrate the transition
between the smelling box and the vinaigrette which gradually came to the fore
in the 19th century.

Over the centuries the great majority of smelling boxes were made in gold
or silver, though some were in base metals such as bronze and copper; the
Victoria and Albert Museum possesses two examples in pewter. Smelling boxes
in hardstone are relatively rare, but fine pieces are shown in pl. II and fig. 38.

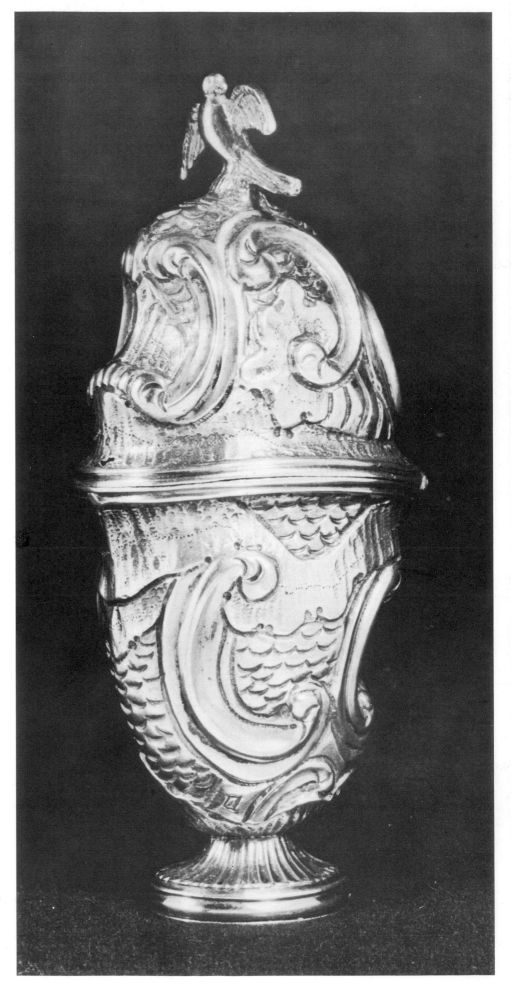

Fig. 37. Smelling box, silver-gilt
enriched with repoussé scrollwork
and scale pattern. Danish, *c*.1795.
574 mm high. *DROM-Schatzkammer*

Fig. 38. Egg-shaped smelling box,
jasper in golden cagework; inscription
on white enamel rim, *Par faveur
croit l'amour!*, and chased ornaments
of flowers, foliage and birds. Release
button set with a diamond. French
(Paris), *c*.1650. 45 mm high. *Otto
F. Ernst, Wiesbaden*

48

Pl. VII. Group of oblong scent bottles with painted decoration and/or gilding. The étui on the left is original. *left* 2nd half of 18th century. 130 mm high. *centre* 3rd quarter of 19th century. 170 mm high. *right* 3rd quarter of 19th century. 135 mm high. All South German. *DROM-Schatzkammer*

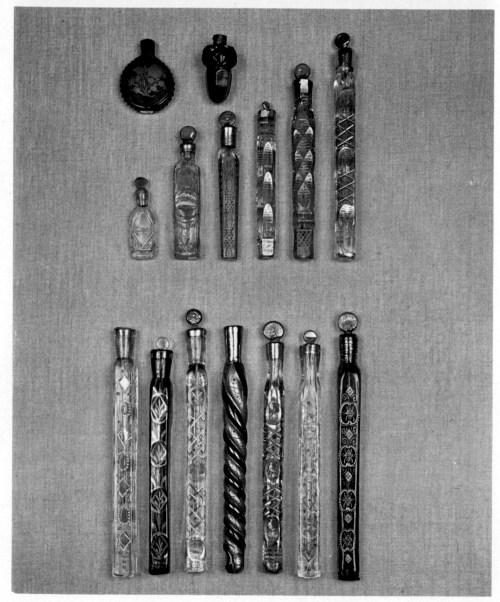

Pl. VIII. Early throw-away scent bottles, sometimes referred to as 'Oxford Lavenders'. *below* The fourth bottle from the left is a unique specimen in the shape of a baroque column, in heavily gilded blue gloss; far right a rare piece in cobalt blue glass with decoration in enamel paint. The small bottle in the upper row, third from the left, still contains its original perfume. German, 1st half of 19th century. *J.M., London.*

USE AND SIGNIFICANCE OF POMANDERS, SMELLING BOXES AND THEIR CONTENTS

The dry perfume substances contained in pomanders and smelling boxes were valued for their alleged medicinal and protective powers, and not, as in the case of liquid perfumes, for any erotic quality. Musk, in early pomanders, was almost invariably used in its natural state, and so would not have had a pleasing smell. Solid perfumes such as musk, ambergris, castoreum and civet were used in pomanders, together with aromatic herbs. Ground spices, such as nutmeg, might also be included in a pomander recipe. Many authors have already pointed out that the pomander's function was twofold, to cover up insanitary odours and also to act, supposedly, as a prophylactic against plague and the many other diseases which raged in those centuries. The first-mentioned use is indisputable, but as for the second, the term prophylactic as it is used today is inapplicable to mediaeval pomanders and their contents. True prophylactic measures, such as innoculation and immunization, are the results of a highly developed medical science and are used only in the prevention of diseases with a known cause.

To understand how mediaeval man could place his trust in herbs and other substances we must try to imagine the spiritual and intellectual climate of the Middle Ages, when popular belief held that demons and evil spirits were the originators of disease, or, at best, that disease was sent by God to test or punish. Mediaeval medicine was a pragmatic art, not based on scientific knowledge. Scholastic dogmatism excluded the possibility of independent research, and turned medicine into a field of dialectics and hair-splitting arguments on the theories of Discorides, Pliny, Avicenna and others. Its methods, as a result of the plethora of ideas and doctrines, were obscure and mysterious.

The search for a universal causality of disease is demonstrated by the attention given to astrological phenomena, which were also of paramount importance in the effecting of cures. Instructions for collecting medicinal herbs were extremely complicated: they could only be gathered by certain persons, in a certain manner, and at a certain time when the astral constellations were favourable. According to astrological botany, certain plant shapes indicated the subordination of those plants to particular planets and other stellar bodies. In addition, the so-called doctrine of signatures dominated medical botany for centuries. According to this theory the intrinsic healing powers of many herbs and fruits were made apparent by their shape or some other visible characteristic; for instance, herbs with yellow sap were held to be antidotes for jaundice. The impressive mediaeval inventory of antidotes, including animal substances as well as herbs, should not be thought of in terms of modern therapy. Many if not most of these antidotes were intended to be effective through their mere presence, through their magic powers to prevent the possession of the body by spirits and demons. Their function was not therapeutic or, in fact, prophylactic but apotropaic (Greek *apotropaios* = averting evil). The contents of pomanders were made up to many different recipes, each tailored to a specific disease or evil, and a different one being ordained for each day of the week.[8] No wonder that those who had the means possessed so many pomanders.

The pomander, in its many shapes and forms, was not regarded as merely the container of these substances, as one might imagine—it was itself of apotropaic significance. Usually, and in its earliest form almost invariably, it was used as an amulet. There is evidence for this in objects which combined an amulet with a pomander, and also in the placing of pomanders together with amulets of all kinds. The first point is demonstrated by a most beautiful 17th-century rock-crystal amulet, surmounted by a globular pomander, which is to be found in the inexhaustible Kriss Collection. (Rock-crystal, in Christian symbolism, signifies the lucidity of Scripture and the virginity of Mary; many

Pl. IX. *above l. to r.* a. Cut overlay perfume bottle in the shape of a boot, Bohemian, early 19th century; b., c. flat lithyalin glass bottle by F. Egermann or imitator; cut and highly polished lithyalin glass bottle by Egermann with ground glass stopper and silver-plated screw-top, both *c.*1830; d. waisted perfume bottle in clear glass, cut on the wheel, with gold mount set with stones and glass stopper under hinged cap, possibly French, early 19th century. *centre l. to r.* e. Cologne or smelling bottle in cameo glass with opaque white cherry motif on light blue ground, with glass stopper and hinged silver cap, made by Thomas Webb and Sons, *c.*1887; f. acorn-shaped perfume flask, English, early 19th century. *below l. to r.* g., h. Two glass scent bottles in *cloisonné* gilt cases, glass probably English, metal-work Chinese, both late 18th century; i. rare combination of perfume bottle and patchbox with a piece of cobalt blue cut-glass set into the hinged silver lid of the box. English (Birmingham), *c.*1785; j. cobalt blue glass scent bottle with inserted silver-mounted enamel panel, probably made in the Birmingham area, late 18th century. All actual size. *J.M., London*

49

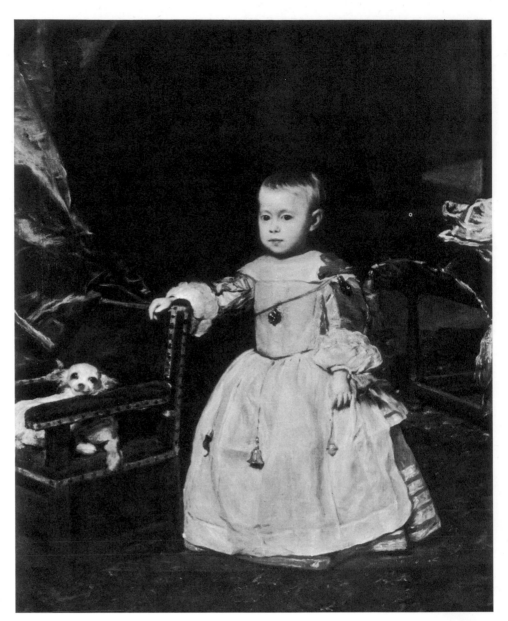

Fig. 39. The Infante Philip Prosper, by Diego Rodriguez de Silva y Velasquez (1599–1660). The ailing boy, aged two, is depicted wearing a smelling box (on his chest) and several amulets (a fica, a silver-mounted coral, a gold-mounted globular piece of jade and a golden apotropaic bell). *Kunsthistorisches Museum, Vienna*

amulets in rock-crystal are extant.) The second point is well illustrated in figs. 28 and 39. Amulets were most carefully designed, since here too certain shapes and materials were considered antidotes for specific evils and diseases. A kind of comprehensive insurance could be taken out, by wearing several amulets at once, as may be seen from the veritable battery of apotropaic objects with which the young princes are armed. In the painting of the Hapsburg prince (fig. 28) we can identify a Marian monogram, a fica, a badger's claw, a horn suspended by three chains, a bell, and the pomander. (The apotropaic use of the bell is not well known—because of its friendly character in warning of impending danger it was widely used as an amulet.) In the rather sad painting of the Infante Prosper (fig. 39) we see a smelling box (on his chest), a fica (left shoulder), a piece of metal-mounted coral, an apotropaic bell and a jasper-sphere (jasper signifies strength and is the astrological symbol of Leo).

The shape of the pomander is itself significant. Throughout the Western World the apple has been the symbol of eternal life and vigour, and the attribute of goddesses. We have only to think of the numerous representations of the Virgin Mary as Queen of Heaven holding the orb which is clearly modelled on the apple; one of the most exquisite examples is Francesco Botticini's Virgin Enthroned (*c.* 1470) in the Musée du Louvre. In the hand of temporal rulers it symbolizes might and power. The walnut shape of the *Betnuss* (fig. 31) is also symbolic. The walnut tree was introduced into transalpine countries by the Romans, and according to the doctrine of signatures the peculiar shape of the walnut shell and its convolutions represented the skull and the brain. The same interpretation was made for the stones of peach, apricot, cherry and nutmeg, which were made into amulets, often with beautiful gold or silver mounts. Nutmeg was also mounted as a pendant love token.

The English herbalist William Cole (*Adam in Eden*, 1657) wrote:

> . . . the Kernel hath the very figure of the Brain, and therefore it is very profitable for the Brain and resists poysons; For if the Kernel be bruised, and moystned with the quintessence of Wine, and laid upon Crown of the Head, it comforts the Brain and head mightily.

Animal shapes too are significant. The symbol of the fish is to be found throughout the ages and across cultures, and its place in art, religion and magic is a subject in its own right. In some cultures the fish signifies fertility, and in the Western World it is the symbol of the Christian faith. In Mediterranean countries fish amulets were, and still are, widely used as sexual symbols. The fish shape has been used for smelling boxes and scent bottles throughout their history (figs. 35, 40, 41, 42, 43), but by the 19th century, of course, the shape was used for aesthetic rather than symbolic reasons.

Land snails, because of their ability to withdraw into their shells in adverse conditions, were regarded as symbolic of spring and resurrection. Snail-shaped smelling boxes (fig. 36) were used as an apotropaic against the plague. Sea-shells appealed to the imagination of our ancestors on account of their layering and attractive structures, and were widely used as amulets and smelling boxes. Shells were sometimes seen as a symbol of the female genitals, and the numerous amulets made from cowrie shells do not leave much to the imagination; spice and smelling boxes of this type are very rare. The mythological importance of the egg hardly needs to be explained: as symbols of fertility egg-shaped objects are widely used as Easter gifts (see figs. 38, 44).

The most common shape taken by amulets is that of the hand; it was also used for scent bottles and smelling boxes. It is quite impossible to narrate every aspect of hand symbolism—not to mention gesticulatory meanings—the history of which goes back to the Palaeolithic period and still plays its role in the Islamic world. Only one particular form concerns us in this context, the so-called *fica*, that is, a clenched fist with the thumb protruding between the index and second finger. The name alludes to the fig (Latin *ficus*) and the symbol has a distinctly erotic connotation, the position of the fingers representing the immissio penis. As a gesture it is interpreted as signifying sexual intercourse, and from the Middle Ages has been regarded as an insult to the person to whom it was directed, unless used discreetly as a means of love communication. It was also, on the other hand, used to ward off evil spirits. How an erotic symbol, or more explicitly a representation of the genitals, could have acquired this second function has led to much conjecture. One theory put forward[9] refers to the treatise of a French writer, Jacques Ferrans, 'De la maladie d'amour ou mélancholie érotique' (1623), which stated that spirits would emanate from a person in love and be transmitted into the body of the beloved object, where they would engender like feelings of love. To prevent this occurrence, Roman ladies are supposed to have carried an obscene figure (*fascinum*) suspended from a necklace. The question remains curious. In the 17th and 18th centuries, when the fear of demons and evil spirits was waning, scent bottles in the form of the fica no doubt conveyed the erotic meaning the symbol stood for originally. Besides the superb examples in fig. 45 I have only seen one other specimen (in the Bayerishes Nationalmuseum, Munich). Hand-shaped amulets and similarly shaped bottles not showing the fica are common and were intended to bring riches or good luck (fig. 46). The symbol of the skull needs no explanation.

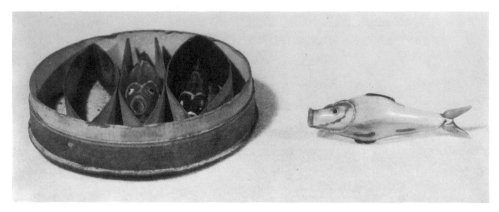

Fig. 40. Enamel smelling bottle in the shape of an articulated fish. Italian, 17th century. Approx. 140 mm long. *Kunsthistorisches Museum, Vienna*

Fig. 41. Cardboard box containing perfume samples used by travelling salesmen for the products of Grasse; lamp-blown glass phials. French, first half of 19th century. Phials 56 mm long. *Musée d'Art et d'Histoire, Grasse*

Skull-shaped pomanders were either one of the many forms of memento mori, or amulets—often the grinning version—to ward off evil spirits (fig. 29).

The most subtle use of the apotropaic qualities of a substance is the burning of incense; during the so-called Dark Ages this was not confined solely to the rites of the Church. Mixtures of powdered herbs and resins for this purpose were prepared according to complicated instructions, in which even magic numbers played an important role—only units of 3, 7, 9, 21, 49 or even 99 of the same or different ingredients were effective. Incense burning was an integral part of early Christian worship and it is noteworthy that when St. Augustine declared all sensual pleasures to be sinful he excepted the enjoyment of pleasant fragrances.

BRÛLE-PARFUMS

From time immemorial people have attempted to perfume the atmosphere around them, with fragrant flowers or with pungent scents emitted from incense burners and perfume lamps, also known as *brûle-parfums*. And today, with the renewed interest among the young in oriental religions, the joss-stick is easily obtained in the West. Incense has a long history, going back to the sacrificial rites of pagan peoples. These were later Christianized, but always retained a half-mystic, half-practical purpose, and are still part of Roman Catholic rites today. Later came its profane application in the palaces of the 18th century, where it was used both to cover up insanitary odours and to satisfy people's olfactory appetites.

Incense plays an important role in Hindu worship and funeral rites, and is used by Buddhists and Moslems. There is plenty of historical evidence, supported by the existence of a multitude of receptacles, for the burning of incense for religious and profane purposes in China and Japan. The practice spread from the Orient to Ancient Greece and finally to Rome. It was only hesitantly introduced into Christian worship. It was during the post-Constantine period, that is, after A.D. 400 that the censer gradually made an appearance; mediaeval inventories listed it as thymaterium, turibulum or incensorium. In the 13th century it was certainly used universally in worship.

The function of the censer, the burning of aromatic resins or perfume,

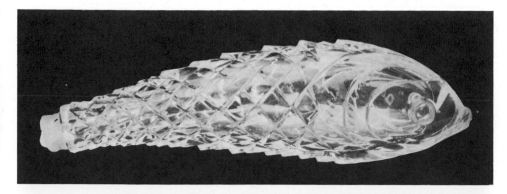

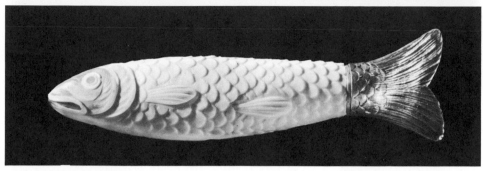

Fig. 42. Scent bottle in the shape of a fish, cut on the wheel and unmounted. English (Daniel and Lionel Pearce), late 19th century. 130 mm long. *DROM-Schatzkammer*

Fig. 43. Cameo glass scent bottle in the shape of a fish; fleshy red ground with grey-blue overlay. The tail fins, worked in silver, act as a screw-on stopper. English (Thomas Webb and Sons), late 19th century. Approx. 95 mm long. *Leslie Scott*

dictated its basic construction: the heat source, usually glowing charcoal, is placed in a lower compartment and above it the incense itself. There must be an outlet in the upper part to enable the volatile substances to escape as the censer is swung. Throughout the Middle Ages the art of the metalworker created a wealth of shapes, many of which were imitated in porcelain during the 18th century. By this time the incense burner had become an elaborate *objet d'art* in its own right, as illustrated by the pieces in figs. 47 and 48. The foremost producers of incense burners in Europe were the factories of Meissen, Ludwigsburg and Nymphenburg in Germany and Chantilly, Mennecy and Saint Cloud in France. Incense burners should not be confused with potpourri vases, often described as *brûle-parfums* (pl. III).

The use of bird and animal shapes in censer designs, either suspended on chains or free standing, is common to many cultures: the Kunstgewerbe-museum in Hamburg has some Japanese examples in the form of cranes, and the inventory of Mainz Cathedral treasures mentions similar birds in silver which were placed on either side of the altar in the mid-13th century. During the following centuries boat-shaped censers suspended from chains, known from contemporary inventories as *navis* or *navicula*, were widely used. A most beautiful English example in silver-gilt, dating from the 14th century and formerly belonging to Romsey Abbey, can be seen in the Victoria and Albert Museum, and in the same museum there is another piece, early 16th-century, bearing the inscription *Dirigatur sicut incensum oratio mea*. One can assume that the vessels generally known as aquamaniles were occasionally used as incense burners in church services.

It is not surprising to find that they were already being produced during the early days of the Meissen factory, some in Böttger's stoneware. They took the form of seated Buddhas and were known, paradoxically, as 'pagodas'. The piece in fig. 48 reflects this contemporary Oriental taste, but it represents a slightly different category, the perfume burner or perfume lamp.

In a censer the scent is released by actually burning or heating the substance, which is usually a resin. In the case of the perfume burner or lamp, perfume is burnt on a wick, on the same principle as for any spirit lamp. The perfume in question is a cologne (*eau de Cologne, eau hongroise, eau de Portugal*, or special preparations sold as *eau à brûler* or *eau pour brûler*). In the 19th century a more

Fig. 44. *right* Egg-shaped enamel scent bottle painted with floral motifs and trellis-work. English (South Staffordshire), *c.*1770. 40 mm high. *left* Lidded enamel scent bottle, painted with a pair of lovers, with silver mounts. Paris, mid-19th century. 80 mm high. *DROM-Schatzkammer*

Fig. 45. Two enamel-decorated scent bottles in the shape of forearm and hand (fica), one in opaque white, the other in dark blue clear glass; pewter mounts and stoppers. South German, late 17th/early 18th century. 102 mm high. *Musée d'Art et d'Histoire, Grasse*

Fig. 46. Double scent bottle in the shape of a hand grasping a shell-shaped bottle; opaque white glass with colour streaks. French, 18th century. 85 mm high. *Musée d'Art et d'Histoire, Grasse*

Fig. 47. *Brûle-parfum*. Group of *putti*, in white porcelain, in four parts. German (Nymphenburg, with Auliczek pressmark AC), early 19th century. 220 mm high. *DROM-Schatzkammer*

Fig. 48. Perfume burner in hyalith glass with gilt decoration; mounts of gilt metal and enamel. Bohemian, 2nd quarter of 18th century. 185 mm high. *R., Frankfurt-Main*

Fig. 49. *Brûle-parfum* in clouded glass. French (Lalique), early 20th century. 210 mm high. *R., Frankfurt-Main*

effective method was introduced, by which a piece of spongy platinum was placed over the wick as a catalyser. Once the platinum was red hot the flame was blown out and the platinum, situated in the rising stream of alcoholic vapour, remained incandescent as long as there was sufficient fuel in the container. The resulting fumes escaped from variously shaped outlets, as in the censer (figs. 48, 49). Another method for 'sweet fumigation' was the burning of scented paper ribbons, also called perfumed spills, in specially designed vases. The perfumed paper was chemically treated to allow for slow, flameless combustion.

The multitude of Victorian pastille burners, in the shape of cosy little china cottages, should also be mentioned; the Victorian drawing room is inconceivable without them. In principle they do not greatly differ from the censer: a mixture of charcoal, gum arabic and benzoin was lit inside the cottage and the perfume vapours escaped through the chimney.

The most subtle way of scenting a room, short of using live flowers, is the use of the potpourri, a mixture of dried scented flowers kept in an open bowl. This ancient custom is still widely practised. The mixtures now available in perfumery shops usually consist of rose petals, lavender (flowers and leaves), pieces, of orris, cloves, cinnamon, Myrtus, pimenta and other dried flowers. The lidded potpourri vase (pl. III) is thus a sibling of the flower vase.

Chapter 3
Glass Bottles

Most of the scent containers used throughout the centuries have been made of glass. Egyptian, Greek and Roman scent flasks have survived to our day and can be admired in museums and private collections all over the world. Glass-making in Western Europe saw a gradual decline during the first millenium, but a revival of the art came about in 12th-century Venice. There the substances essential for glass-making were to be found, and the town could boast a great artistic tradition. Most importantly, Venice was Europe's gateway to the East. It was undoubtedly the contact with the Near East, especially with Damascus, a great centre of glass-making, which lent early Venetian glass its beauty, notably in enamel decoration, a technique which was highly developed in Islamic glass-making.

One of the greatest achievements of Venice—for the purposes of this book the various glass-houses of the region must go under this name—was the production of clear glass, which, for its resemblance to rock crystal, was named *cristallo*; the production of such glass only became feasible in the 16th century, after the discovery of the decolourizing properties of manganese. One will search in vain for scent bottles among the vast quantity of Venetian glass extant dating from before the middle of the 17th century (few exist, and I have only seen one which could date from this period, mentioned below). The reason for this is quite simple: the vogue for liquid perfume as we know it today dates roughly from the mid-17th century. Yet in fact few scent bottles were made of glass, even then, since glass was a cheaper substitute for more costly and more desirable materials such as rock crystal, other hardstones and precious metals. The scent bottle was, after all, an accessory used by people familiar with luxury and high fashion. The picture was the same throughout Europe: in France the rejection of glass in favour of more precious materials is well documented; drinking glasses were never to be found on an aristocrat's table, only goblets made of other materials. This was the case until the end of the 18th century.

The few glass Venetian scent bottles which can be traced are of great interest, especially on account of their decoration. The flask in fig. 50 (one of a pair) is decorated with gilded gesso, which has stood the test of time well. Only a few pieces of Venetian glass with this type of applied decoration are extant and not many in such a fine state of preservation. The lack of sufficient material for comparison, and the fact that no similar example has yet been identified in a painting or engraving, makes it difficult to date this pair exactly. In the opinion of most glass historians, they could have been made in the second half of the 16th century.

The commonest type of scent bottle generally attributed to Venice, or at least to Venetian *émigré* craftsmen working in Germany, is represented by fig. 51. The flattened pear-shaped bottle is decorated with trailing which is completely fused into the glass surface, and often, as in this example, the trailing is 'combed' into a zig-zag pattern. A bottle in the shape of a sea creature (pl. IVb) is of the same origin. The coloured streaks, some in aventurine, on the cream-white surface were achieved by sprinkling chips of coloured glass on to the surface of the marver plate, over which the molten gather of glass attached to the blowing iron was rolled before further blowing. The applied prunts are a typical feature of Venetian glass of the 17th century. Surprisingly, I have never come across a scent bottle of this period with true *latticino* decoration, but there are a number of *latticino* flasks in various collections which may pass as toilet water bottles.

Occasionally one finds small barrel-shaped vessels, the surfaces of which are completely covered with bright splashes of red, yellow, blue, brown and white. Vessels of this type vary greatly in size, but smaller examples of these so-called *tonnelets* were certainly used as scent bottles. This decorative technique was a Venetian innovation of around 1600, as is testified by a fine tankard in the Moritzburg Collection, but it was subsequently copied throughout Europe and therefore scent bottles in the *tonnelet* shape and showing this bright decoration could have been produced in Spain, Holland or France. A few authors have referred to glass with this type of decoration as *millefiori* glass, a somewhat unfortunate term as it is already used to describe glass of a completely different style and period. As for the barrel shape, scent bottles have been made in this shape throughout history: there is a fine Roman specimen from the Rhineland made in the 2nd century A.D. in the British Museum. A superb 17th-century German example is seen in fig. 52.

There are a number of glass scent bottles with enamel decoration in various European museums. They are all similarly decorated with flowers and birds (see fig. 53) and in most instances are labelled as Augsburg products. Axel von Saldern, however, has cast doubt on this attribution by pointing out that the Museo Vetrario in Murano has a portrait of Osvaldo Brussa, a Venetian glass painter, holding a beaker which is similarly decorated.[10] The mounts of these bottles—metal rims into which a stopper is fitted, giving a tight closure—differ both in material and style from those of contemporary German bottles (mainly *Schnapsflaschen*). It is remarkable, however, that these early 18th-century enamelled bottles should have been produced in Venice where the art of glass enamelling had been abandoned almost a century before. Among the enormous amount of 17th- and 18th-century German enamelled glass only a few scent bottles are to be found (fig. 45).

Let us at this point take a cursory look at the technique involved in glass enamelling. It is not to be confused with painting, also termed cold painting, on glass. The paint used for enamelling is made up of a mixture of finely ground coloured glass and a flux. When the painting has been executed the vessel is heated in a kiln, and the paint becomes fused into the surface of the glass. This technique produces a decoration far more durable than cold painting.

The vagrant life of the Renaissance glass-makers is well known, and Venetian craftsmen worked in various parts of Europe. The first man to make fine

Fig. 50. Bulb-shaped glass scent flask, with applied gesso ornament. Venetian, mid-17th century or earlier. 140 mm high. *R., Frankfurt-Main*

quality glass in England was a Venetian, Giacomo Verzelini (1522–1606) of Murano, who, after working for some years in Antwerp, produced what was subsequently called Verzelini glass during the last quarter of the 16th century. How closely the secrets of glass-making were guarded in Venice, and how they came to be known to the outside world, is a fascinating story which has been told by various authors.

Glass-making in France was greatly influenced by Venetian styles: some of the glass made at Nevers was actually described as '*du Petit Murane de Venise par Thomas Corneille*'. With regard to scent bottles it is virtually impossible, with the exception of some mould-blown flasks, to attribute any of the few known 17th- and early 18th-century pieces to a particular glass-house. In the Musée des Arts Décoratifs in Paris one can see a number of superb late 17th-century bottles in which the body, either of glass or ivory, is covered with coloured *verre églomisé* beads so arranged as to simulate needlework and form coats-of-arms or figurative representations such as birds, and pastoral or mythological scenes. (A fine piece is illustrated by Kate Foster in *Scent Bottles*, pl. 25.) The

Fig. 51. Scent bottle of a flattened pear shape; greenish glass with combed opaque white trail-work and pincered glass-trailing along the edges. German or Venetian, early 17th century. 95 mm high. *J.M., London*

59

Fig. 52. Barrel-shaped glass scent bottle with applied threads; pewter screw-top. German, 2nd half of 17th century. 105 mm high. *DROM-Schatzkammer*

elegant bottle illustrated in fig. 55, however, is more remarkable for its mount than the actual glass body shape.

The two gourd-shaped bottles in pl. V are intriguing. Both the glass and the style of the pewter screw tops suggest that they could be attributed to the Paul Perrot glass-house at Orléans, and were made towards the end of the 17th or early in the 18th century. If this is so they certainly represent one of the earliest examples of a silvered glass vessel.

The story of glass-making in Spain has been told by A. W. Frothingham.[11] When it comes to searching for scent bottles the field is rather barren. On stylistic grounds the piece illustrated in fig. 56 could have been produced in one of the Spanish glass houses of the Granada province. The British Museum has two late 17th-century bottles with an extraordinary abundance of coarse applied pincered decoration, one in greenish-yellow, the other in olive green glass, which may have been used for scent or snuff. Like most Spanish glass of this kind they appear to be more of a joke than a practical proposition. Onc can almost see in them the Spaniard's disdain for glass as a material. The decoration, eccentric in the extreme, renders these bottles completely im-

Fig. 53. Two oblong scent bottles in *Milchglas*, decorated in enamel colours with a cavalier on the front and flowers on the reverse; gilded neck. Bohemian, 18th or early 19th century. 80 mm and 60 mm high. Scent bottle in clear glass, decorated in enamel paint; gilt metal mount and screw-top. Venetian, early 18th century. 90 mm high. *R., Frankfurt-Main*

practical. Both are illustrated in Frothingham's monograph (fig. 518). Another sturdier Spanish bottle in dark green glass can be seen in the Victoria and Albert Museum.

However exciting it would be, there is no room here for delving deeply into the history of German glass. When studying glass from the 17th to 19th century one should bear in mind that German glass also comprises glass often referred to as Bohemian or Austrian. The strong Venetian influence is already discernible in glass of the 15th century, and when we come to glass of the 17th century we cannot always be sure, at least in the case of scent bottles, that a 'Venetian' piece was not actually made in a South German glass-house. Typical indigenous German glass was of a green or brownish colour, and termed *Waldglas*. Among the various items of utility glass made of this metal we find medicine bottles and also, since the dividing line between medicinal and cosmetic preparations or perfume is often blurred, the so-called *Rosolen* flasks. (*Waldglas* is discussed in an earlier chapter on account of its association with *eau de Cologne*.) Further illustration of the close relationship between medicinal products and those for the toilette is provided by the curious bottles in fig. 57 which were used for either toilet water or scented cosmetic oil. They differ from the ordinary pewter-capped medicine bottles only in that they have a glass figurine, at the bottom and fused to the base, in the form of a gargoyle or heraldic beast. They were a glass blower's *tour de force*, true to the tradition of *Scherzgläser* (trick or joke glasses) of which German craftsmen were so fond. The German phials contained in a casket, in fig. 58, are also interesting.

Perhaps one of the greatest German contributions to glass technology was the invention of ruby red glass. A fair number of 17th- and 18th-century pieces made in this material are extant; one is illustrated in pl. VI. A very elegant gold-mounted scent bottle, in cut and polished ruby glass and of the flattened tear shape, can be seen in the glass gallery of the Victoria and Albert Museum. Similar bottles, overlaid with gold cage-work, occasionally appear on the market.

For more than a century, beginning at the close of the 17th, South German and later Bohemian glass-houses produced numerous scent bottles in *Milchglas*,

Fig. 54. Bottle in the shape of a hunting horn; clear glass with combed opaque white trailings, gilt metal mounts and screw-top. French, late 17th/early 18th century. 118 mm high. *Musée d'Art et d'Histoire, Grasse*

an opaque white glass (*milch* = milk). White glass was a Venetian invention, most probably the result of attempts to imitate Chinese porcelain which had become known in the West in the 15th century. It was achieved by the addition of tin oxide, arsenic or bone ash to the glass mixture. One of the earliest Venetian pieces, dating from the early 16th century, a spherical vessel (wig-stand?), is in the British Museum.

Venetian scent bottles in opaque white glass are extremely rare and we cannot be sure whether or not the streaked bottle shown in pl. IVb is of Venetian origin. The purist may object to *Milchglas*, since it gives the impression of being glass in disguise, but it enjoyed public favour over a long period and provided a superb vehicle for gilding and enamel decoration. Early German *Milchglas* scent bottles are also exceedingly rare. A fine example is in the Houbigant Collection (Paris); it is about 125 mm. high, of the flattened pear shape and decorated with floral motifs and figures (a pair of lovers?) in fine gilding.[12] Less rare but by no means common are the German enamelled *Milchglas* scent bottles of the late 18th (fig. 53) and early 19th century (pl. IVj). Bottles like the one in pl. IVj are sometimes offered as 18th-century items; the costume of the cavalier, however, suggests an early 19th-century date. At this point two other opaque white scent bottles should be mentioned, although they are of a later date (pl. IVh, i). Pl. IVh shows a bottle of a transparent bluish white, which should be described as an opaline bottle; the pure white glass bottle in pl. IVi could easily be taken for porcelain by the less knowledgeable. It is superbly decorated in an imitation Chinese style.

There is yet another fine decorative technique which, originally invented by Dutch craftsmen, was developed to great .artistic heights by German artists, most notably Johann Schaper, active in Nuremberg 1640–70: I refer to *Schwarzlot* decoration. In this process the glass surface is covered with a mixture of copper oxide and black enamel pigments, and the intended design is then scratched out, as in etching. Fine *Schwarzlot* glass is rare; the only early scent bottle with this type of decoration that I have seen is shown in fig. 59. *Schwarzlot* painting was revived by Bohemian glass workers in the late 18th century and during the 19th it was applied to glassware of all kinds, including toilet water flasks.

One could write a complete history of glass based on the scent bottle, and one would find the time-honoured methods of glass-making reappearing in many countries down the centuries, with additional technical innovation. Glass-blowing was invented shortly before the birth of Christ, probably in the eastern Mediterranean (Phoenicia). Early free-blown flasks were shaped with wooden tools in the process of blowing, a technique which has not changed in the course of two millenia. We know of most beautiful blown vessels from the beginning of the 1st century which clearly demonstrate that the new technique was soon employed for artistic purposes, and that the makers of the vessels had gained a true understanding of this pliable material. Glass bottles from the latter part of the 1st century bear the stamp of the place of origin (e.g. Sidon) and/or the name of the makers, the most frequent being Ennion, Meges, Artas and Ariston. Strangely enough, all fourteen vessels signed by Ennion, except three, were found in Northern Italy. This is one indication of the speed with which the art of glass-blowing spread throughout the Empire. The migration of glass-makers rather than parallel development is certainly the explanation for the creation of similar pieces in widely separated parts of the Roman world.

As for mould-blown vessels for perfume, we know of mould-blown bottles from Syria, head-flasks from Cyprus, a fish-shaped bottle from Provence (Arles) and flasks of various shapes from the Cologne area. All mould-blown bottles of Roman origin were blown into bipartite moulds, and in many instances the mould marks are clearly visible, especially at the base. Shells and grape clusters are common shapes. In Rome, head-shaped bottles were very much in fashion: they are mainly janiform head-vases, sometimes showing

Fig. 55. Gold-mounted glass scent bottle of a flattened tear shape. Goldsmith mark Jacques Meyboon, Paris discharge mark for 1732–38. French, 1st half of 18th century. 98 mm high. *Sotheby & Co., London*

Fig. 56. Flask in clear colourless glass with opaque yellow embellishments. Spanish (?), 18th century. 100 mm across. *Victoria and Albert Museum, (Crown Copyright)*

63

Fig. 57. Cylindrical bottles of bright green glass, with inserted glass figures, pewter mounts and screwtops. German, 17th/18th century. 110 mm and 100 mm high. *Leslie Scott*

Fig. 58. *left* Box in the shape of a book containing six glass phials for essential oils, each 20 mm long. Florentine, early 19th century. *centre* Casket with lacework containing a small glass scent bottle (20 mm high). German, late 19th century. *right* Cardboard box containing eight phials in clear glass, with paper etiquettes. French, 1790. Phials 50 mm high. *DROM-Schatzkammer*

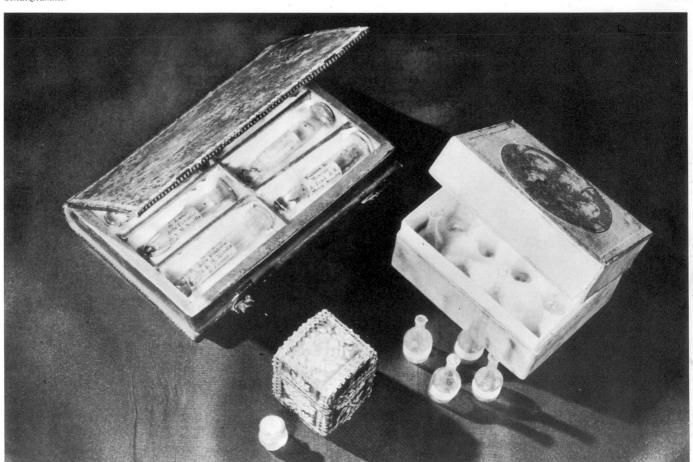

Pl. X. Four-part cologne bottles in green glass with cut stoppers in clear glass, in a gilt basket-like mount. French, 2nd half of 19th century. 140 mm high. *DROM-Schatzkammer*

Pl. XI. Two scent bottles in blue opaline glass. German, 2nd quarter of 19th century. 75 mm and 55 mm high. *DROM-Schatzkammer*

Pl. XII. *Art nouveau* scent bottle in red-tinged glass, with acid-etched flower motif (poppy); base and shoulder with gilt metal mounts. French (Daum?), *c.*1910. 142 mm high. *DROM-Schatzkammer*

Pl. XIII. *Art nouveau* gold-mounted scent bottle in overlay glass, by Tiffany of New York. 57 mm high. *Sotheby & Co. (reproduced by kind permission of H. Ricketts)*

Fig. 59. Glass scent bottle and stopper; spherical body (with facet-cutting) drawn into a long neck cut with shallow flutes. Schwarzlot decoration (hunting scene and leaf motifs). German, 1st half of 18th century. 145 mm high. *Kunstgewerbemuseum, Cologne*

identical addorsed faces, sometimes different ones, one serious, the other smiling. In these janiform flasks the mould-mark separates the faces on either side. There are also a number of bottles in the form of a complete single head. Originally head-shaped bottles must have played an important part in religious rites, but in latter-day Rome they were used as a vehicle for caricature, depicting well-known figures with greatly distorted features. Their German name, *Schustergläser* (cobblers' glasses) comes from a famous example representing Nero's court jester, who was a shoe-maker by trade. In the Römish-Germanisches Museum in Cologne there is a negro head-bottle, again with the features somewhat caricatured. After more than thirteen centuries the famous glass-house of Paul Perrot in Orléans made mould-blown bottles based probably on Roman examples (see fig. 60), and these pieces, not uncommon in our museums, were for some time considered to be, in fact, of Roman origin. The large number of intact Roman perfume bottles in museums and private collections all over the world reflects the important role which aromatic substances played in the daily life of the times, and the quantities of these substances that were used.

It is not always easy to distinguish between free-blown and mould-blown Roman glass. Some flasks were probably mould-blown first and then further expanded by free-blowing. In some bottles the mouth is connected to the shoulders of the body by delicate ingeniously twisted handles, often in different coloured glass, attached after the moulding process had been effected. Decora-

Fig. 60. Pair of mould-blown glass bottles in opaline glass, in the shape of human heads: *left* with pewter mount and screw-top, *right* silver-mounted. French (Orléans), c.1675. *J. M., London*

tions of glass threads trailed around the neck occur occasionally.

I have not come across mould-blown scent bottles of the Dark Ages and the Venetian period, but in 17th-century France a great number were made at the Paul Perrot glass-house. Compared with other French bottles of the period, the Perrot products are slightly crude but one cannot deny them a certain old-world charm. The most common type is of the flattened tear shape with fleur-de-lys or flower motifs in moulded relief. The bottles are usually deep amber in colour—blue ones are rarer—but sometimes in clear glass. Most specimens have a simple pewter screw-cap (pl. V, fig. 61), but finer pieces—this seems to apply only to bottles made of clear glass—have silver mounts at the foot and neck. The foliate chased silver stopper is tightly fitted and sometimes connected to the mount by a silver chain (as in fig. 61). The shell-shaped bottle seen in pl. IVc is a rare example; it is made of thick amber-coloured glass blown into a bipartite mould and decorated with opaque white glass threads. These were trailed round the bottle when it was removed, still hot, from the mould, and fused into the surface by reheating in the gloryhole. The head-shaped mould-blown bottles attributed to Perrot are usually made of blue milky glass, but there is one black glass specimen in the Musée des Arts Décoratifs. Most of these bottles are pewter-mounted, silver mounts being the exception (fig. 60).

These Orléans mould-blown bottles undoubtedly represent the first mass-produced glass scent bottles in history. The use of perfume in France in the late 17th century was no longer exclusive to the nobility, the emerging bourgeoisie creating a demand for it and a market for a cheaper type of scent bottle. Their relative frequency in museum collections bears witness to this. An octagonal mould-blown beaker in the British Museum shows that Perrot made other kinds of vessels also.

Mould-blown glass is basically utility glass and can never be ranked among the aristocrats of the glass-maker's art. The technique lends itself to the production of containers on an industrial scale and it is but a step from mould-blown to pressed glass, the latter technique not being of great interest to us in the context of antique scent bottles. Nevertheless, its wide industrial application during the 19th century led to a serious decline in cut-glass, especially since both mould-blown and pressed glass were to simulate the entire range of patterns invented by the glass cutter. Before dealing with this subject, mention should be made of a curious group of flacons which were probably made by Messrs. Paris in Bercy around 1833 and traded as *'flacons de cheminée'*. They

Fig. 61. Mould-blown pear-shaped glass bottle with fleur-de-lys decoration in high relief; tightly fitted silver stopper and silver mounts. French (Orléans), c.1675. *J. M., London*

Fig. 62. An original cardboard box containing six mould-blown phials, each for a different perfume. Sold by L. T. Piver, perfumer, Paris, 1857. Phials 45 mm high. *J. M., London*

Fig. 63. *above* Double scent bottle in original case. Dark green glass with silver-gilt mount, studded with coral 'gems' and hall-marked 1872. English. 117 mm long. *J. M., London. below* The poor relation. Mould-blown double scent bottle in green glass, with gun-metal caps screwed directly onto the glass. English, 2nd half of 19th century. 138 mm long.

Fig. 64. Mould-blown flask in neo-gothic style; brick-red glass. French (Launey, Hautin et Cie.), mid-19th century. 70 mm high. *J.M., London*

consist of a bottle in the shape of an ornate round pedestal (blown into a four-sided mould) and a mould-blown stopper (bipartite mould) in the shape of a bust of some great man (examples are known for Goethe, Napoleon and Voltaire). All of them are in opaline glass in shades ranging from milky white to sky-blue. Although considered by some authorities to be ink pots it is more than likely that they were used for cologne or even perfumes.

To return to the imitation of the cut-glass article, one rarely finds mould-blown scent bottles of this kind, although there are a small number of cylindrical double scent bottles of which the surfaces are decorated with a hobnail pattern (fig. 63). But there are many mould-blown cologne and toilet water flasks to be found, few of them meriting the collector's attention.

The moulded scent and cologne bottles made by Launey, Hautin et Cie. in Paris between 1830 and 1840 are outstanding, both for their high quality and as curiosities. Based on Gothic and Romanesque architectural elements, their decoration appears in high relief and exhibits an extraordinary degree of clarity of detail. Not many of these survive, but a fine piece complete with mould-pressed stopper is to be seen in fig. 64. Like most of their kind they are thick-walled and made of dark red glass (similar in tone to the colour of sealing wax). This firm did not confine its designs to expressions of the Gothic revival; when thumbing through its pattern books one meets with Oriental shapes and motifs, Etruscan floral ornament, rococo scrollwork and symmetrical cut patterns. Most bottles of this type (and glassware in general) were hand-finished, that is, mould-marks or other adhesions on the surface were cut away on the wheel and the entire surface then polished.

PAINTED GLASS BOTTLES

The purist rejects on principle the decoration or colouring of glass, but in the case of oil-painting on glass, even if one has no opinion as to the aesthetic rights or wrongs of it, one cannot fail to be aware of the unsuitability of this form of decoration from a purely practical point of view. Its inappropriateness is immediately obvious when one sees the pitifully worn decoration on objects the very function of which necessitated frequent handling. To hazard an opinion as to its visual success even when well preserved, I would say·that the oil-paint revolts against the glass surface and the resulting contrast is too harsh to be pleasing.

Nevertheless, painting on glass has a long history reaching back to Venetian glass of the 16th century when oil-paint was occasionally used as a cheap substitute for enamel. Examples of 17th-century German glass are also known, partly painted with flower motifs in order to conceal cracks or impurities. It was only during the 17th century and part of the 18th, however, that glass painting was practised on a larger scale and mainly for the decoration of mirrors. Here also the fashion may have come about through the necessity to camouflage flaws in these costly objects. No less an artist than Van Huysum produced a fair number of flower paintings on glass panes. Glass vessels, mainly wine bottles, painted in the Dutch fashion of the same period, frequently appear on the market. Also noteworthy are the apothecaries' bottles and jars, mainly of the 18th century, decorated with oil-paint or other paints.

The revival of painting on glass which took place in the 19th century is attested by German and Austrian glasses of the Biedermeier period, but it represents, so to speak, an artistic cul-de-sac in this otherwise very exciting period of technological and aesthetic innovation in glass. Although oil-paint was used in most instances, the artist also employed the technique of lacquering, adopting a style similar to that found in contemporary snuff boxes by Stobwasser of Brunswick and others. I have never seen a single scent bottle decorated in this manner but there are a variety of both scent and toilet water bottles in which the entire surface is painted either in marbled or mottled patterns so that at first glance one does not identify them as glass bottles at all. Items of this nature are often dismissed by the connoisseur of fine antiques, but they are nevertheless interesting objects which were not intended as masterpieces: however cheap labour was in those distant days there was nevertheless a limit to the amount of work that could be spent on something which was intended to

Fig. 65. Free-blown scent bottles in clear glass with flashed edges (red on yellow), decorated in cold painting in the style of German peasant art. Bohemian, early 19th century. 30–50 mm high. *Parfumerie Fragonard, Grasse*

69

be sold cheaply. The rather humble bottles depicted in fig. 65 were made somewhere in Bohemia and are most probably products of a cottage industry. Each bottle in this collection is slightly different in size and shape. The edges are flashed in red or yellow, leaving a circular panel rather naively painted with motifs denoting the contents. Snuff bottles of similar design, but usually somewhat larger and without a ground stopper, were made in Bohemia and southern Germany.

The bottles illustrated in pls. VII and VIII were made to hold scent for the not-so-rich and were also intended to appeal to the tourists flocking to famous spas such as Karlsbad (now Karlovy Vary) and Marienbad from all parts of Europe. Intended as disposable bottles, they are the earliest representatives of a type of scent bottle to be met with fifty to seventy years later all over Europe. The reader is no doubt familiar with the species shown in pl. VIII; these long slender bottles, often traded in this country as 'Oxford lavenders', are usually crudely made, square in cross-section, and fairly heavy in the hand, both size and weight being out of all proportion to their capacity. Indeed, in many cases the lower third is of solid glass and the scent is contained in a hollow tear-shaped cavity that tapers towards the constricted neck.

Some experts consider that these bottles are English, but I believe they were made in quantity in southern Germany (Bayerischer Wald and Fichtelgebirge) and then exported to Bulgaria to be filled with rose water. The ornamentation, which certainly displays a distinctly central European flavour, adds weight to this theory. The bottle on the left in pl. VII is the earliest—and indeed the most charming—I have seen; 18th-century specimens are very rare. Although dealers of doubtful reputation try to pass them off as 18th-, 17th-, or even 16th-century, most of them were produced from the late 18th century almost to the end of the 19th.

Clear glass examples are the most common, but green and also blue bottles are found, the latter varying in tint from light blue to dark cobalt. The earlier specimens are the more crudely cut with either shallow horizontal grooves or a criss-cross pattern, and with additional ornamentation in the form of geometrical gilded patterns or painted floral motifs. The decoration not only embellishes the bottle but also serves to mask imperfections in the thick-walled glass.

Among the many 'proletarians' of this group, choice specimens worthy of even the finest collections may be found, as we see in the exquisitely decorated deep blue bottle, far left in the lower row in pl. VIII, and the rare twisted bottle in the centre of the row; the latter, reminiscent of a baroque column, is also in blue glass and heavily gilded. Almost all bottles of this type have a conical ground-in stopper; specimens complete with stopper are rare and more expensive, and the unsuspecting collector should beware of false stoppers. The genuine stopper will fit tightly, and is almost invariably circular and flattened; its gilding, even if only traces remain, should be seen to match that on the neck of the bottle.

Painted glass vessels were also made in England, to a limited degree, in the second half of the 19th century. A rather interesting example is shown in fig. 66, and I have seen another one depicting a pond with a pair of swans in the rushes. The scarcity of this type of bottle would suggest that not many were made.

EIGHTEENTH-CENTURY ENGLISH GLASS BOTTLES

We may pass over the mediaeval period in England if our interest lies in the study of fine glass. Sixteenth-century *émigré* glassmakers from Lorraine were responsible for the first quality glass in this country and it was another foreigner, Giacomo Verzelini, already mentioned, who in this country made glass comparable to the Venetian product. In the late 17th and throughout the 18th

opposite page
Fig. 66. Disc-shaped glass scent bottle with sky-blue ground overlaid with clear glass and painted decoration; silver mount and hinged lid over a cork stopper. English, *c*.1880. 90 mm high. *J. M., London*

71

century, however, English craftsmen could hold their own with their Continental counterparts, making glass the quality of which was second to none.

As for scent bottles, we search in vain for English specimens dating from the 17th century or earlier. There is, however, a group of enigmatic bottles the origin of which has not so far been convincingly established. I refer to the examples in fig. 67 (right) and fig. 34. What makes these bottles especially interesting is the fact that they represent the earliest known examples of multi-purpose bottles in glass. They combine a scent or smelling bottle (the glass body) with small boxes (set into the central hollows), the use of which is open to conjecture; they may have been containers for patches or rouge. Some have additionally a small pomander fitted to the silver top (fig. 34 left and centre). It cannot be ruled out that the foot in at least some of these bottles was meant to be used as a seal. The bottles are uniformly of the flattened shape seen in the illustrations and somewhat crudely cut in rather shallow horizontal steps. A rarer variety has a square body as opposed to the round or oval-shaped bodies illustrated here.

The dating of these bottles is facilitated by the English silver coins used in some of them as push-on lids to the lateral compartments. Fig. 67 shows an example with a Vigo sixpenny piece, dated 1703, on one side, and a small silver portrait medallion of Queen Anne on the other. Another bottle which I have seen has a monogram and the date 1714 engraved on the bottom of the foot-mount. But the earliest example known to me is the one in fig. 34; its original box bears a dedication label—in English—dated 1691.

All these facts would in themselves indicate English workmanship but their most prominent feature, namely the cutting, contradicts the findings of glass historians: whereas the art of glass-cutting had reached high standards and was

Fig. 67. *left and centre* Two souvenir scent bottles with silver mounts and an engraved silver inset panel. Probably Dutch. 92 mm and 99 mm high. *right* Cut-glass smelling bottle with central hollow on either side to take a lidded compartment; front lid made of a Vigo sixpenny piece of 1703, reverse lid (*centre*) made from a silver medallion depicting Queen Anne. English, 1703 or earlier. 80 mm high.

practised on a large scale in Germany throughout the 17th century, no cut-glass of any quality seems to have been produced in England before 1715 and then most probably by German craftsmen working in this country. If one could prove beyond doubt that the scent bottles in question were actually made, and not merely mounted, in England, the accepted date for the introduction of cutting would have to be pushed back by at least twenty-five years. That proof can indeed be furnished by chemical analysis: a spectroscopical examination of the bottles shows lead to be a major constituent in the glass. Over the entire period to which these bottles can be attributed (from 1691 or earlier to 1715) lead-glass was an English monopoly—it was first produced by George Ravenscroft around 1675. According to Robert Charleston[13] the first place on the Continent to acquire the 'arcanum of making lead-crystal *à la façon d'Angleterre*' was the German glass-house of Lauenstein in Brunswick-Lüneburg (before 1744). The same author states, however, that some lead glass, but of a much lower lead content, may have been produced by the Bonhommes of Liège at the end of the 17th century, a source which we can safely exclude as far as these scent bottles are concerned. That the bottles were made by a London glass house is highly probable since the first illustration of one appears, among many other items, on a few maps of the General Atlas issued by George Willdey in 1715. There it reads:

> Advertisement: This map of the world and ye rest of ye quarters and several other maps . . . also sold by George Willdey at ye great toyshop next to ye Dog Tavern in Ludgate Street for 8 pence. Where are made to the greatest perfection all sorts of spectacles, reading glasses, Telescopes, Perspective glasses, Microscopes and whatever is curious of this kind.

Fig. 68. *left* Etui in tortoise-shell set with silver *piqué*-work, containing scent bottle and silver funnel. English (?), 18th century. 85 mm high. *centre* Cut-glass scent bottle with silver mounts and engraved gold inset medallion. German, 1st half of 18th century. 75 mm high. *right* Glass scent bottle with silver mount and engraved silver inset panel. Dutch, mid-18th century. 100 mm high. *front* Glass scent bottle harnessed in pseudo-baroque metalwork (silver-plated). German, *c*.1870. 60 mm high. *DROM-Schatzkammer*

Fig. 69. Selection of perfume flasks. *above* Three pieces in clear glass, two engraved with the owner's name. English or Irish, 2nd half of 18th century. 97 mm, 89 mm and 92 mm high. *below l. to r.* Bellow flask; bottle in finely corrugated clear glass, decorated with pincered trailings; gimmel flask; bottle of a flattened oval shape. English, late 18th/1st half of 19th century. 125 mm, 93 mm, 100 mm, and 97 mm high.

Where also yᵉ Curious may be furnished with all sorts of Cuttler's wares and curious Toys in Gold, Silver, the true Bath and others Metul's . . .

The cloudiness of the interior surface of almost all bottles of this type, resulting from the corrosive action of the smelling salts, suggests that they served as smelling bottles rather than scent flacons. Whether there is any connection between them and the slightly similar Dutch and Bohemian bottles seen in figs. 67 and 68 is impossible to establish.

Larger perfume and smaller cologne bottles were so frequently used as smelling bottles that one finds it difficult to distinguish one from the other, except in cases where a smelling bottle is fitted with a special spring closing device. True smelling bottles are usually thick-walled and often deeply cut to make the material less conductible of heat, since they are usually carried on the person or held in the hand. Smelling bottles came into fashion during the second part of the 18th century, had their heyday in the 19th, and are still used to some extent today. Smelling salts were of various compositions, the most active ingredients usually being ammonia, phenol, eucalyptol, menthol and similar invigorating substances. The addition of scent—usually lavender—made the pungency more agreeable.

One of the most prolific makers of smelling bottles was R. H. Barrett of The Oval in the Hackney district of London. He advertised certain smelling bottles, among others, 'made in white and coloured glass, plain and fluted . . . with screw metal cap fitted with an indestructible washer'. One type of washer consisted of a small glass ball within the screw cap which was pressed against the concavely shaped metal mount of the bottle.

Snuff bottles may also be mistaken for scent bottles, but generally snuff bottles have larger mouths to facilitate refilling and most of them are indeed more capacious. There are borderline cases, it is true; some of the flasks in fig. 69 (top row and 2nd on left below) may well be snuff bottles. The magnificent metal flask in fig. 70 may also belong to this category, or it may even have been used as a priming flask.

To return to our discussion of scent bottles, the second half of the 18th century was a period when English craftsmen created a plethora of certain bottles of unprecedented beauty and elegance, hardly surpassed elsewhere; I refer to those in opaque white and cobalt blue glass. In the past these kinds of glass have been known as Bristol Enamel and Bristol Blue. Much scholarship and time-consuming searching of archives in connection with stylistic comparison has shown that both categories of glass were made in various parts of the country—but mainly in South Staffordshire—besides Bristol. The work of Robert Charleston and J. Bedford is outstanding in this field, and some of their most important contributions are listed in the bibliography.

We do not know with any certainty why English glass-houses embarked on making opaque white glass. There was, of course, a considerable influx of enamelled *Milchglas* from Germany, and the English gentleman on the customary Grand Tour became acquainted with the Venetian product. Also true porcelain was there to be imitated. Perhaps the ultimate motive was the fact that opaque white glass did not come under the crippling Glass Excise Act of 1745 which imposed a tax on glass made in England and Scotland.

In spite of the fact that lead-glass was used, and not soda glass as on the Continent, English glass-houses soon succeeded in making an opaque white

Fig. 70. Cast silver bottle with neo-classical motifs. French (Rheims), 1776. 83 mm high. *J. M., London*

Fig. 71. Opaque white glass bottle with gilt decoration and inset glass cameo; gold screw-top with spiral repoussé waves, over a glass stopper. English, 1770–1780. Approx. 72 mm high.

opposite page

Fig. 74. Opaque white glass bottle with gilt decoration representing an exotic bird between trees, and boulders in the foreground; the reverse shows a pagoda motif. English, 1770–1775. Approx. 72 mm high.

Fig. 75. Blue glass bottle of an elliptical shape with formal flower decoration in enamel colours. English, 3rd quarter of 18th century. 72 mm high.

Fig. 76. Blue glass bottle of elegant elliptical outline, slightly flattened, with gilt decoration showing a neo-classical lidded urn bearing the owner's initials, surrounded by bird and plant motifs. English, 1770–1789. Approx. 100 mm high.

Fig. 77. Blue glass bottle with cut edges and gilt decoration: on the front, a structure, rather than a building, within a formal border, and a peacock on the reverse. English, 1770–1775. 42 mm high.

Fig. 72. Opaque white glass bottle cut all over with shallow facets, with chinoiserie decoration in enamel colours and gilt borders to shoulders and sides; gold screw-top with spiral repoussé waves, over a glass stopper. English, 3rd quarter of 18th century. Approx. 90 mm high.

Fig. 73. Blue glass bottle of a flattened pear shape, cut all over with shallow facets and decorated in enamel colours; gold screw-top with spiral repoussé waves. English, 3rd quarter of 18th century. Approx. 72 mm high.

glass which, at its best, was indistinguishable from porcelain. The aesthetic objections pertaining to this sort of glass have already been indicated, yet in the case of scent bottles it is eminently more suitable from a practical point of view (and this applies to some extent also to the blue glass under consideration) than the clear colourless metal. Many, or indeed perhaps most, of these English bottles were used as smelling bottles, and thus the corroding effect of the ammonia was perfectly concealed by its colour or opacity. Even if they were used as perfume bottles the opacity of the glass would have been of great advantage since light is detrimental to perfume. A small number of bottles, nevertheless, were made in colourless glass. A superb specimen, similar in shape and design to the one in fig. 71 can be seen in the Schreiber Collection (Victoria and Albert Museum), and the two bottles in pl. IXi and j show that both blue and colourless scent bottles could have been made by the same firm. Besides the blue and white one finds similar bottles in green glass, and also an amethyst variety of the true Bristol blue.

Leaving aside the technical details, let us confine ourselves to the decorative treatment of these small treasures which represent one of the highlights of the glass-maker's art as manifested in England, and which form delightful diversions among the accumulations of drinking vessels usually found in collections of English glass. In these bottles it seems as if decorators of English glass have shed the native inhibitions apparent in other English glass of the period, however superb their basic material and technological skill. One cannot help but wonder why almost all writers on English glass have paid so little attention to these creations, but concentrated on the classification of drinking vessels.

Compared with contemporary Continental bottles of the rococo period, most English bottles in both opaque white and blue glass are cut in a rather restrained manner. Often there is merely a levelling and notching of the edges (pl. IXi and j), and occasionally bottles of a similar shape are decorated with

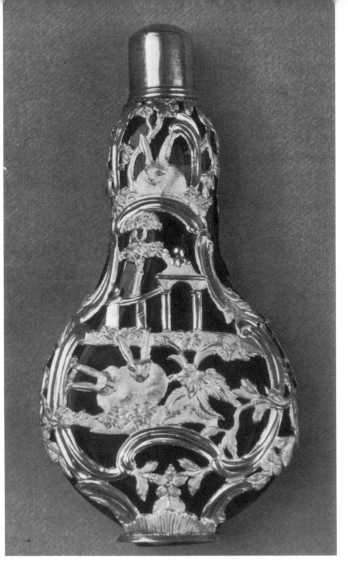

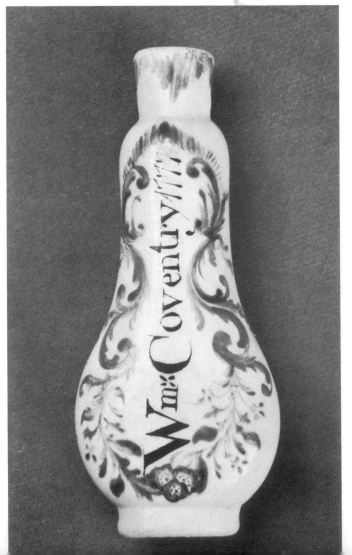

notched shallow flutes. The most common type, however, is the one in which the entire body is cut with shallow facets, with remarkable regularity, as seen in figs. 72 and 73. It has been suggested that the cutting away of so much glass surface served the purpose of rendering the bottles lighter, thus reducing the amount of excise duty calculated by weight. I doubt whether the labour costs involved in this tedious process would have made the exercise worthwhile and I am inclined to attribute it to aesthetic aims rather than accountancy.

The decoration of these 18th-century glass scent bottles shows a marked similarity to earlier and contemporary decoration of both porcelain and enamel and one might assume that at least some of the craftsmen were engaged for the decoration of both. The similarity of the style and motifs in bottles decorated with coloured enamel paint with those of actual enamel ware supports the argument that most of them were produced in the heartland of the enamel industry rather than in Bristol. Amongst the enamel-painted opaque white scent bottles, pieces decorated with scenes in monochrome are as rare as they are beautiful; a superb piece decorated in the chinoiserie style so favoured at this period is in the glass gallery of the Victoria and Albert Museum. In many coloured and opaque white bottles the enamel painting decoration is heightened by gilding—and indeed, a large number of them are embellished by gilding only (figs. 74–76).

Whereas the identity of craftsmen working in enamel paint remains unknown —most of the attributions to Michael Edkins have been proved wrong[14]—in the case of gilding many a fine piece of work can be attributed with great certainty to the porcelain decorator James Giles (1718–80), or at least to painters working for him in his atelier in Berwick Street, Soho.[15] On stylistic grounds the bottles in figs. 71, 74 and 77 belong to this category. In most of these bottles the pattern of the gilding is seen to be correlated with the cutting, resulting in a most pleasing effect (figs. 71, 77).

opposite page

Fig. 78. Blue glass bottle of a flattened pear shape overlaid with elaborate gold cagework, probably by James Cox. English, 1775–1785. Approx. 70 mm high.

Fig. 79. Blue glass bottle of a flattened pear shape overlaid with elaborate gold cagework, with watch and compass, signed James Cox. English, 1770–1785. Approx. 105 mm high. *Christie, Manson & Woods Ltd.*

Fig. 80. Glass bottle overlaid with elaborate gold cagework, with inset enamel medallion, probably by James Cox. English, 3rd quarter 18th century. Approx. 70 mm high.

Fig. 81. Opaque white glass bottle decorated with flower sprays in enamel colours and bearing the owner's name and the date 1777. English. Approx. 77 mm high.

Fig. 82. Same as fig. 81 but with a different owner's initials and the date 1785. English. Approx. 77 mm high.

Fig. 83. Superbly engraved flat oval-shaped glass bottle (the engraved parts also gilded), showing owner's initials. On the reverse there is a rhombic panel of diamonds cut in shallow relief. Silver push-on top. Irish (Waterford), 1795–1800. 110 mm high. *J.M., London*

The cobalt blue and amethyst-coloured bottles in figs. 78–80 enclosed in gilt metal cages of openwork, many of which are attributable to James Cox, are almost in a class by themselves. The artist's choice of motifs makes the example of cagework in fig. 78 especially delightful.

Dated English scent bottles of the 18th century are rare, but sometimes one finds a date on a less sophisticated type of opaque white bottle, usually together with the name or initials of its owners (figs. 81, 82). They were undoubtedly made to order and one should always bear in mind that this type of bottle could have been made earlier than the date on it suggests. It is this kind of bottle, also, which sometimes has the transfer-paint decoration associated with cream-coloured earthenware from the Liverpool region.

The production of glass scent bottles during the second half of the 18th century on this side of the Channel was by no means confined to bottles in opaque white and coloured glass. On the contrary, an even greater number of flasks in flint-glass were made, most of them characterized by an unmistakable range of more or less flattened shapes, either rectangular or elliptical in outline

Fig. 84. Selection of variously cut clear glass bottles of the type frequently found in ladies' needle-work boxes or compendia; one (*top left*) with a panel to take the owner's initials. Most probably Irish, late 18th/early 19th century. 81 mm, 85 mm, 90 mm, 107 mm, 113 mm and 96 mm high.

Pl. XIV. Scent bottle in the form of
an owl, in labradorite; eyes ruby,
gold mounts. German, c.1810.
65 mm high. *DROM-Schatzkammer*

Pl. XV. Gold repoussé scent bottle,
with enamelled flowers and animals,
the foot in the shape of a seal
(cornelian). French, mid-18th
century. 63 mm high. *Victoria and
Albert Museum (reproduced by kind
permission of H. Ricketts)*

Pl. XVI. Hardstone double scent
bottle in the form of a boy holding a
lamb; neck and base with gold
mounts. English (?), *c.*1760. 89 mm
high. *Victoria and Albert Museum
(reproduced by kind permission of
H. Ricketts)*

Fig. 87. Glass scent bottles. *left*
Snake-shaped bottle in yellowish
glass, wheel engraved. Perhaps
English. 92mm high. *below, 2nd from
left* Bottle in the shape of a sea-horse,
in opaque white glass with coloured
stripe. English. 64mm high. *right*
Bottle in the shape of a mandolin,
in red glass with gilding. Perhaps
English. 67mm high. The other phials,
one in deep blue, two in a striped
clear glass, have dates in trailed work.
All English. 48mm, 49mm and 49mm
high. All early 19th century.

opposite page
Fig. 85. Close-up of a perfume flask
of the same shape as in fig. 86,
showing a wheel engraved portrait of
William IV. English (Pellatt and Co.),
2nd quarter of 19th century.
100mm high.

Fig. 86. Perfume flask in elaborately
cut glass with cameo in the shape of
clasped hands; cut mushroom-shaped
stopper. English (Pellatt and Co.),
early 19th century. 100mm high.
J. M., London.

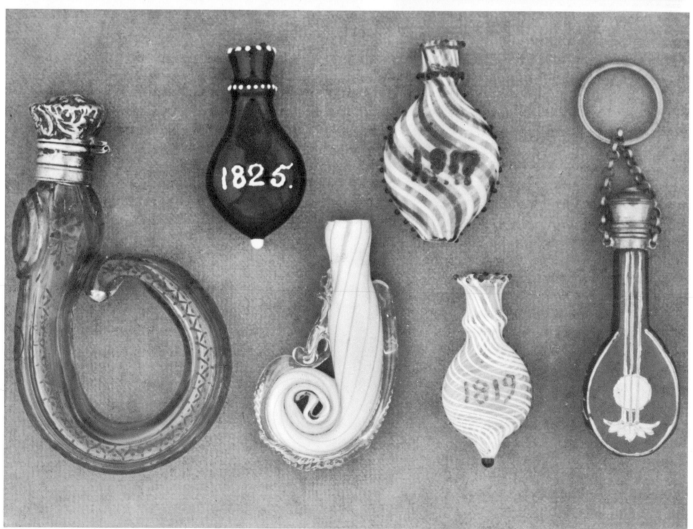

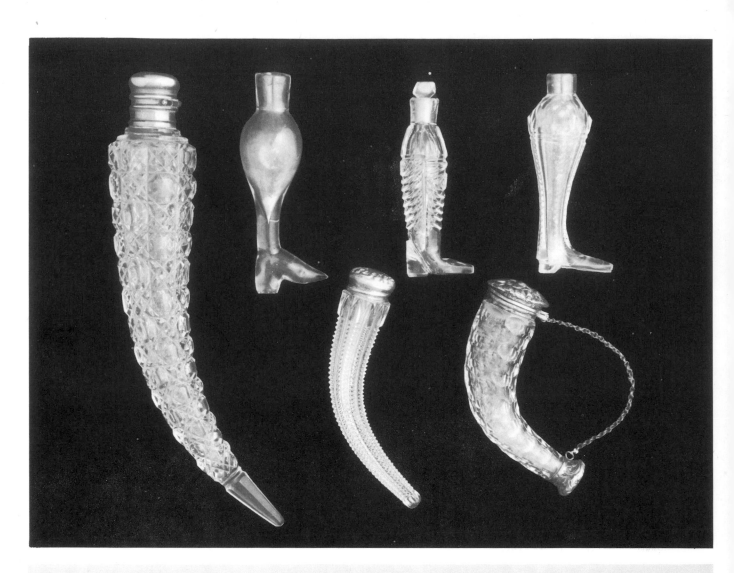

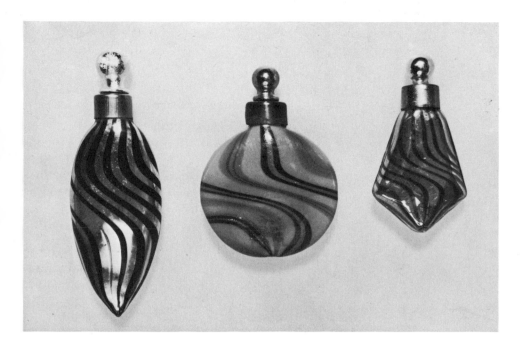

(see figs. 69, 83, 84). Scent or cologne bottles of this nature are always represented in dressing or needlework cases of the period, as may be witnessed by the visitor to the Brighton Museum where a superb collection once owned by Mrs. Fitzherbert, the morganatic wife of George IV, is to be seen. Earlier examples of such bottles are plain and thick-walled, and sometimes bear wheel-engraved names and dates (fig. 69, top row); later ones (c. 1785 onwards) are usually cut and engraved. Many of these bottles are superb examples of the cutter's mastery of his art and, as can be seen in our illustrations, display almost every conceivable pattern that can be realized by the wheel.

The question of their origin cannot always be resolved with certainty but we must assume that most of these bottles were made in one of the Irish glass centres where there was a boom in production after the British Parliament passed the Glass Excise Act of 1745. Since the production of cut-glass in England, however, did not actually cease, it is virtually impossible to attribute scent bottles to Irish or English glass-houses. Only in the case of a few documented bottles (referred to as vials) can a safe attribution to Irish glass-houses (Waterford and Cork) be made.[16] On stylistic grounds, the fine example in fig. 83 is certainly of Waterford origin and many of the others were most likely made there also. Space does not permit lengthy discussion of this matter, but I should point out that in the absence of documentary evidence only comparison of cutting patterns and shapes will enable us to opt for Irish provenance: the old story that Waterford glass displays a bluish tinge has long ago been proved a myth. Any collector wondering about the origin of his own prized specimens should adopt the philosophy of an outspoken lady of my acquaintance: 'When I am enjoying a really splendid meal I don't give a damn about the site of the kitchen.'

Despite the various excise acts, fine cut-glass scent and toilet water bottles were produced in England during the early 19th century. The leading manufacturer of this genre of bottle was Apsley Pellatt, whom we shall meet again in connection with cameo incrustations. Fig. 85 shows a close-up of the intaglio portrait on one of his scent bottles, the shape of which is virtually identical with the one in fig. 86. In most instances members of the Royal family are depicted, and often one encounters the portrait of Queen Adelaide, wife of William IV. The portrait engraving is almost invariably surrounded by a stylized honeysuckle pattern and nearly all bottles of this type are signed 'Pellatt & Co., Patentees'.

Throughout the 19th century, particularly after the excise duty on glass was

Fig. 90. Group of silvered glass pomade bottles with blue (*left and right*) or multicoloured (*centre*) striation; tightly fitted glass stopper, extending into a long rod. Italian, 19th/20th century. 78 mm, 55 mm and 52 mm high. *J.M., London*

Fig. 91. Silvered pressed glass bottle in the shape of a birdcage. English (probably Sowerby and Co.), obscured pressmark of 1872. Approx. 70 mm high.

opposite page
Fig. 88. Glass scent bottles. *left and below* Horn-shaped cut-glass perfume or smelling bottles. The one on the right has a vinaigrette at the wider end. 2nd half of 19th century. 180 mm, 102 mm and 94 mm long. *above* Blown boot-shaped perfume bottle, 18th century, and two bottles of the same shape in cut-glass, early 19th century. 97 mm, 78 mm and 81 mm high. All English.

Fig. 89. Group of smelling bottles in white opaline glass (*left*), turquoise blue (*centre l.*) and ruby red (*centre r. and right*). All with silver-gilt mounts, one with an inset portrait medallion of Queen Victoria. The one on the right has a vinaigrette base signed C. S. Mordan and Co., S.M. and hall-marked 1874. English, 2nd half of 19th century. 93 mm high.

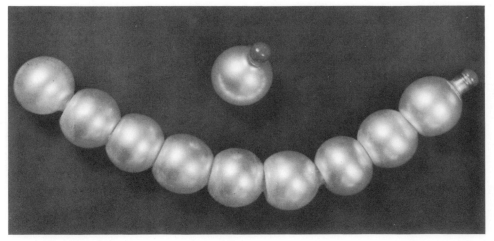

lifted in 1845, scent bottles were produced in considerable quantity by various English glass-houses, notably at Nailsea near Bristol and in the Stourbridge area. With the steady increase in trade between Britain and the Continent after the Great Exhibition in 1851, trade which in the case of glass was a two-way affair, bottles were introduced from abroad and also Continental techniques were adopted by English glass-houses (e.g. overlay and *millefiori* glass). In the absence of documented pieces or factory records it is often quite impossible to tell the English product from bottles made in Germany or France. Thus some of the overlay bottles (pl. IXa) which are labelled Bohemian may well have been made at Stourbridge. Only a thorough chemical analysis can determine provenance, should any collector be anxious for certainty. Two groups of scent bottles are particularly conspicuous during this period: double scent bottles, through their sheer quantity, and cameo glass bottles on account of their artistic quality. Both categories will be dealt with below.

Other bottles which were probably made at Stourbridge, many of them bearing Birmingham hall-marks on their mounts, are seen in figs. 87–89. The old-established firm of Richardson (John 1725–1818, Joseph 1751–1841, Joseph II 1796–1884, Benjamin 1802–87) was outstanding among the Stourbridge manufacturers. The mid-19th-century vogue for Venetian glass led to the making of aventurine-like glass (fig. 106 *left*) and *latticino* glass. The bottle in pl. IXf may be of Stourbridge origin, but the sea-horse-shaped flacon in fig. 87 most certainly is. Among the many colourful trifles in glass, such as walking sticks, tobacco pipes, hunting horns, rolling pins, gimmel flasks, etc., which are labelled Nailsea, one occasionally finds scent bottles. Most of these gay lamp-blown flacons are of a flattened pear shape with opaque (white or coloured) stripes and the date, and sometimes the owner's initials also, trailed over the surface (fig. 87). Without repeating the long story which has been narrated in most books on English glass, I would remind the reader that the term Nailsea Glass, like the term Bristol Glass must be regarded as the indication of a type of glass rather than of its place of manufacture. Glass of this nature was made in glass-houses all over the country as well as in the Bristol area, and for latter-day collectors it must be stated that it can still be produced on the lamp in 1974.

The Victorian craze for silvered glass is also reflected in a few scent bottles of the period. The best-known makers of this sort of glass, using the so-called Drayton method of silvering (patented in 1848), were Messrs. Hale Thompson of London. The scintillating silvered flasks in fig. 90 are of a much later date; their extended tapering glass stoppers indicate that they were used for pomade rather than for liquid perfume. A silvered bottle in pressed glass, the hideousness of which is only matched by its uselessness, is seen in fig. 91. The most recent silvered specimen I was able to trace (fig. 92) can only be described as remarkable; it is an example of what happens when the advertiser takes over from the glass-maker.

CRYSTALLO CERAMIE BOTTLES

The embedding of ceramic objects in glass was first attempted towards the end of the 18th century, and was one of the most original innovations since Roman times. Certainly there was no historical precedent for this technique. The physical properties of glass render the inclusion of alien material technically very difficult. Glass and metal are not compatible; even the fixing of metal mounts to glass present problems, as every craftsman attempting this is aware. Coin glasses had, of course, been made a century earlier but the silver coin was almost invariably contained within a bubble, usually in the knob of the stem. There are only a few instances of a coin fused into the glass.

Although the American collector will be familiar with the term 'sulphides', the English enthusiast uses the term '*crystallo ceramie*' and will immediately think of his countryman Apsley Pellatt (1791–1863) in this context. The technique in question was, however, pioneered in France. Pellatt's merit rests on the fact that he was responsible for its refinement and was the author of a book on the subject. Some sources maintain that Bohemian glass-makers produced cameo incrustations early in the 18th century, but there is no documentary evidence for this, nor are there any objects extant which could safely be attributed to Bohemian glass-houses of this period. The earliest known example of a ceramic medallion embedded in a glass object (and this is not a scent bottle) is in the Musée National de Céramique at Sèvres, and is dated 1796. The quality of this piece suggests that experiments in the technique must have been carried on for years before this date. There are two more pieces in the same museum, one of which is a beaker with inserted ceramic busts, which can with certainty be dated 1798. The busts are signed P. B. and were produced at the factory of H. B. Boileau in Gros-Caillou, near Paris. The two main exponents of the *crystallo ceramie* technique in France were Desprez and Pierre Honoré Boudon de Saint-Amans; both were connected with the Sèvres porcelain works at one time or another. Desprez is the more important; we note that around 1773 he was employed at Sèvres as a chemist, together with Leconte, but it seems that he also took a serious interest in the artistic side of porcelain-making. Some sources refer to him as a '*sculpteur de première classe*'. In 1793 he founded his own firm at 2 Rue des Récollets-du-Temple, and catalogues of successive years show him to have been a manufacturer of porcelain medallions and plaques ('*sculpteur fabricant des camées de porcelaine*'). It is not known whether *crystallo ceramie* was yet produced at this stage.

It is only in 1819, when Desprez's son's name appears in a trade almanac, that the process is mentioned, being described as an '*Assortment de médailles dans l'intérieur du cristal*'. To what extent the fine creations of this period can be attributed to the father or the son it is not possible to ascertain. The quality of the pieces which bear the signature 'Desprez' (also 'D. P.', 'Desprez à Paris', or 'Desprez, Rue des Récollets-du-Temple no. 2, à Paris') suggests that years of experience must have been invested in these achievements. Anyone who has seen his pieces will certainly not agree with the judgement of some authors who feel that they are inferior to Apsley Pellatt's work.

The other French exponent of cameo incrustations, the versatile P. H. Boudon de Saint-Amans (also known as the Chevalier de Saint-Amans) was less successful than Desprez but his life and work are better documented. In March 1818 he was granted a privilege of five years' duration for making cameo incrustations. From this document we learn of the mixture for the cameo (two parts porcelain, two parts frit, one part china clay from Dreux and three parts pulverized crystal glass) and also the method of its embedding. Whether Saint-Amans produced scent bottles is not known; most of his work is unsigned, a regrettable fact which also applies to his compatriots producing cameo incrustations with varying degrees of success, e.g. Dartiques and Martoret.

In England Apsley Pellatt, at the age of twenty-nine, was granted a patent for his process of *crystallo ceramie*, and protection for fourteen years. It is not known to what extent he was influenced by the French attempts in the same technique. The main ingredients of his vitreous stoneware cameos were china clay and super-silicate of potash, and the cameos were mould-shaped, fired and often finished by hand to bring out the finest details of the original sculpture. The embedding of the cameo was a rather dangerous process: it was inserted through a cut into the red-hot glass bubble at the end of the blow-iron, then closed by reheating the bubble in the glory hole. The bubble was collapsed around the cameo by sucking the hot air out of it through the blowing iron. How this could have been carried out without resulting in injuries to the craftsmen is hard to imagine. The incrustation of cameos into the walls of vessels such as scent bottles or beakers was done by pressing them gently into the surface of the vessel and then covering them with an adequate quantity of molten glass. The resulting unevenness of the wall was compensated for by elaborate cutting. The amount of wastage in the process caused by broken or displaced cameos must have been considerable and explains the high cost of these interesting objects. Later, in 1831, Pellatt registered a patent for press-moulding glass with inserted cameos, but since no scent bottles were produced by this method it need not concern us here.

The introduction of *crystallo ceramie*, in France as in England, was by no means accidental but a logical consequence of the vogue for cameos. The idea was not new: portrait modelling as an art had already been practised for more than two thousand years, but in the second half of the 18th century renewed interest in the classical world led to the desire to collect classical cameos and intaglio gems, and also created a great demand for reproductions. From this it was only a step to the commissioning of portrait medallions depicting contemporary celebrities. To the English reader the names of Josiah Wedgwood, James Tassie and John Flaxman spring immediately to mind; on the Continent the equivalents were J. S. Göttinger of Ansbach, N. Marchant of Rome, and J. F. Reifenstein and Joseph Picter of Vienna. As for France, the two Desprez, father and son, have already been mentioned, but there were others. Desprez used numerous medallions and medals by Bertrand Andrieu (1761–1822), Dumarest and L. Posch. Recently a number of pieces with portrait figures in *crystallo ceramie* came to light in Oslo, among them two scent bottles.[17] The cameo in one of them (fig. 93) represents Eugène Beauharnais, Duke of Leuchtenberg and Prince of Eichstädt, and is taken from a medal cut on the occasion of his death in 1824 by the Austrian Franz Xaver Lösch (1770–1826). The cameo in the other bottle is a likeness of King Carl XIV Johann of Sweden and Norway in the style of a Roman Emperor; it was taken from a medal cut in 1821 by Jean-Jacques Barré (1793–1855). Both these bottles could have been made either by Desprez, whose firm continued until about 1830, or by Baccarat; the quality of all the pieces in the Oslo collection, and others as well, puts a definite stop to the myth, partly created by Pellatt's own rather conceited writing, that French work was inferior to that of Pellatt.

Glass-houses in Germany introduced the technique of cameo incrustation at a much later date; documented pieces for Germany include ones from Zechlin (Prussia) and from the glass-house of Neuwelt (close to the border of Silesia) owned by Count Harrasch, and also from two firms in Goldbrunn near Bergreichenstein (Böhmerwald). There are no instances of cameo incrustations prior to 1826. The attribution of most undocumented glasses with cameo incrustations is, in the absence of a signature, hazardous; moreover, cameo-incrusted glasses were imported from France, and the cutting of glass produced by Bohemian and French manufacturers at the time was similar. Nevertheless, we can assume that scent bottles of this kind must have been made at Harrasch's from 1830 onwards. The quality of cameo incrustations produced by the craftsmen of the Neuwelt factory is so high that one can safely mention them in

the same breath with those of Apsley Pellatt and his French counterparts. By comparison with objects known to have been made there, and on stylistic grounds (the shape of the bottles and the cutting), it seems safe to attribute at least one of the two fine bottles illustrated in fig. 94 to the Harrasch glass-house.

COLOURED GLASS BOTTLES

Continental scent bottles produced during the Empire and Biedermeier periods (the latter corresponding to the Louis-Philippe period in France) exemplify the exuberant character of all fine glass produced during those decades. It is almost impossible to find examples of plain glass, if one discounts utility ware such as beer and ordinary wine glasses. Never before in the history of glass-making was colouring used on such a large scale and in such variety. Without undue generalization it may be said that every single piece was also elaborately cut or, to a lesser extent, engraved.

This is not the place to go into the long history of the colouring of glass; this certainly goes back to Egyptian times. Paradoxically, the great ideal of glass-makers over the centuries had been to get rid of the impurities, which gave rise to unwanted colour during the melting process, in order to achieve a glass similar in appearance to rock crystal. Those makers specifically interested in the art of colouring, on the other hand, aimed at creating a pure coloured glass of even consistency. They required a process which would ensure that the colouring could be repeated at will. There were a number of reasons for colouring glass, some of them quite valid and justifiable, others less so. The imitation in glass of porcelain and other materials was without doubt an artistic cul-de-sac, however pleasing the results in some cases. How one judges colouring on aesthetic grounds is a personal matter and one would therefore not wish to dogmatize on the point. Even the most ardent purist must admit

Fig. 93. Scent bottle with sulphide portrait of Eugène de Beauharnais after Xaver Lösch. French (Baccarat), 1st half of 19th century. *Norsk Folkemuseum, Oslo*

Fig. 94. *left* Scent bottle with sulphide in neo-classical style. Bohemian (Neuwelt), 1810–1820. 135 mm high. *right* Scent bottle with neo-classical sulphide portrait. French or Bohemian, *c.*1820. 60 mm high. *Wella Museum, Darmstadt*

that the interplay of cutting and colouring in certain pieces of glass has a pleasing decorative effect which cannot be achieved in plain glass. In the case of scent bottles we can well imagine that the lady of the period might have a predilection for a certain colour, or require her flacon to match the shade of her outfit or her cologne bottle to match the colour scheme of her dressing-table. There are, however, practical advantages in having a coloured scent bottle. Perfume does not necessarily have an attractive colour, and indeed if the flacon is used as a smelling bottle the corrosion of the clear glass is unsightly. In addition, light causes perfume to deteriorate and dark glass therefore protects this precious liquid.

Coloured glass of any description may be divided into two categories, namely those in which the metal is coloured throughout and those where only the surface has been coloured. Let us first consider the former.

Most red scent bottles are of the very popular ruby colour. This can be obtained by adding either a copper oxide or gold in the form of gold chloride to the basic metal. The latter method has usually been attributed to the famous German chemist Johann Kunkel (c. 1630–1703) and his product is often referred to as Kunkel glass, although this attribution is queried by many glass historians. Kunkel himself writes that the actual discovery of the phenomenon was made by the Hamburg physician Andreas Cassius and that he learned of it in 1676. Kunkel produced superb ruby glass in the Potsdam glass-house of which he was director from 1679–93. Ruby glass was none the less being made at the same time in South German glass-houses. The most interesting aspect of the process of ruby glass-making is that the glass only becomes red after reheating—at first it appears ash-grey. Glass of a deeper red is obtained with copper oxide, and this method was more often used for overlaid and flashed glass. A fine pink-tinted glass is created by the admixture of silenium, an element discovered by Berzelius in 1817.

A number of typical 19th-century red glass bottles are seen in pl. VI.

Blue glass can be obtained by the use of oxides of both cobalt and copper or a mixture of these. Cobalt glasses range from almost black to bright sapphire, whereas copper oxide colours range from sky blue to turquoise and lapis lazuli. Blue glass has a long history. In the 18th century, blue glass of superb quality was made in England, and then during most of the 19th century in Bohemia and southern Germany. Many of the late 19th-century English double scent bottles were made in blue glass.

Fig. 95. Variations on the tear shape. *left* Elaborately cut double-tear-shaped flacon in ruby red glass with gilded and enamel decorations; silver mount and hinged lid. Bohemian. 130 mm high. *centre* Flacon of a flattened tear-shape in deep green glass, cut and polished and gilded with stars; silver mount and hinged lid. Bohemian. 110 mm high. *right* Flacon of an inverted tear shape in ruby red cut-glass; gold mount and top. French. 100 mm high. All 3rd quarter of 19th century. *Wella Museum, Darmstadt*

The admixture of chromium oxide results in green glass (fig. 95, pl. X). Under certain conditions this colour can also be produced by means of copper oxide. Many Bohemian scent bottles and cologne flasks were made in yellow glass, which is obtained mainly by the use of antimony, cadmium sulphide or silver chloride. The shade range extends from lemon yellow—scent bottles of this colour are sometimes in the shape of a lemon as in fig. 96—to amber. Amber-coloured flacons (fig. 97) were first exhibited by Friedrich Egermann at the Prague exhibition in 1829. On the whole, yellow and green glass shows a wider shade range than glass in other basic colours. The flacons and cologne bottles in luminous clear yellow or green glass are not to everyone's taste, but they enjoyed an immense popularity in their day. Their luminosity is due to the addition of small quantities of uranium which was, and still is, mined in western Bohemia. The main manufacturer of these glasses was Joseph Riedel of Polaun who brought them on to the market around 1850. He apparently named his radiant products after his wife Anna, and thus they became known as 'Annagrün' (alternatively 'Eleonorengrün') and 'Annagelb' glasses. The greenish chyrsopras glass should be mentioned in this context. It was first produced in the glass-house of Count Harrasch at Neuwelt in 1831, but scent bottles in this glass are rare. This applies equally to flacons in orange colours. There are, however, many scent and smelling bottles in purple or amethyst-coloured glass (figs. 98, 99) obtained by the admixture of manganese (not magnesia, as is sometimes erroneously stated).

The output of coloured glass in Germany during the first half of the 19th century was quite unprecedented. The fashion soon spread to France where coloured glassware of superb quality issued from the factories of Saint Louis, Clichy, Baccarat, Le Creusot, Choisy-le-Roi, Epinay and Bercy. The similarity in colour and decorating techniques makes it very difficult to give scent bottles

Fig. 96. Group of scent bottles in opaline glass, two in the shape of an egg (white and green), one lemon-shaped (yellow). English, late 19th century. Approx. 60 mm, 63 mm and 50 mm high.

Fig. 97. Collection of cut-glass scent bottles. *above l. to r.* Amber-coloured, 55 mm high; dark amber-coloured, 45 mm high; dark green, 63 mm high; translucent milk white, 68 mm high. *below l. to r.* Bright red, 79 mm high; watery green with gilt decoration, 84 mm high; cobalt blue, 85 mm high; clear vaseline glass, 75 mm high. All Bohemian, 1st half of 19th century.

Fig. 98. Smelling bottles. *above* Blue overlay on clear glass with sharp angular cut patterns. 98 mm and 96 mm high. *centre* Facet-cut red overlay bottle. 125 mm high. *below* Deeply cut thick-walled bottle in purple-violet glass, and deep amethyst-coloured glass bottle with highly polished surface and gilded floral decoration. 70 mm and 90 mm high. English, 2nd half of 19th century. *J.M., London*

Fig. 99. Amethyst-coloured glass bottle, base and shoulder with elaborate silver openwork; hinged silver lid. French, 2nd half of 19th century. 128 mm high. *Wella Museum, Darmstadt*

a French or Bohemian label with any certainty; chemical analysis has not yet been done systematically.

It is essential to be aware of this difficulty when we consider opaline glass since it is usually attributed exclusively to French firms. The term 'opaline' is itself rather vague; it was first used by Baccarat in the early 1820s. The Germans called it *Opalglas* and at Saint Louis it was quite aptly named *pâte de riz*. The term 'agate' also occurs in glass literature, referring to French white opaline. At any rate the term is a general one: strictly speaking it is not possible to draw a clear line between milk glass (especially the German variety and that produced at La Granja in Spain) and opaline. It would certainly refer to a white or lightly coloured glass which is opacified and therefore semi-translucent. If we accept opacity as the main criterion, then all milk glass with a fair degree of translucency may be classified as *verre opaline*. The existence of Venetian examples has been attested: Antonio Neri (d. 1614), a Florentine priest and chemist, wrote about glass of this nature in a peach colour with a blue, green or pink glow. With regard to scent bottles, the earliest known examples in this type of glass are the negro-head flacons made at the Perrot glass-house in Orléans around 1675 (fig. 60) which were discussed earlier. Their basic colour is greyish-white but they show a most beautiful golden-blue opalescence in transmitted light.

We must turn to the German glass-houses of the Bohemian region for the first opaline to be produced in great quantity, most of it coloured (pl. XI). Lemon-tinted opaline was made as early as 1810. Opaque amber glass is recorded for this period, and at the 1835 Vienna Exhibition the firm of Count Buquoy is represented with a glass termed 'opal margaritte'. In his book *Gläser der Empire- und Biedermeierzeit*, G. Patzaurek illustrates (as fig. 234) a cologne flask in the shape of the classical *Rosolen* with a stand in cut opaline glass.

After 1820 there was a noticeable upsurge in opaline production in France, which catered for a fashion bordering on a craze for objects made in this

Fig. 100. Collection of scent bottles mostly in opaline glass. *above* Commercial bottle for 'Ambre de Delhi Babani' perfume, black decoration on gilt surface; flat circular bottle in opaque purple cut-glass; the same shape, in opaque blue glass with gilt metal cage. 46 mm, 37 mm and 42 mm high. *below* Flat circular bottles in opaque white, oily yellow and opaque white glass with silver leaves. French, early 20th century. 45 mm, 42 mm and 32 mm high.

Fig. 101. Pair of perfume bottles in blue opaline glass with gilt formal flower decoration. French, 2nd half of 19th century. 77 mm high. *J.M., London*

92

material. No other country can be credited with opaline of such superb quality, witness its brilliance, consistency of colour and variety of subtle tones such as *gorge de pigeon*, *blue d'outremer*, *bleu céleste*, *gris pigeon* and some of the pinks (fig. 100).

Like all coloured glass, opaline is an ideal vehicle for gilding (fig. 101) and —to a lesser extent—painting in enamel colours. Most pieces of French opaline glass, and this applies especially to glassware for holding perfume or colognes, were metal mounted, the more exquisite ones in ormulu, the cheaper in bronze or brass. The collector should be aware, however, that not all mounted opaline scent bottles are French; bottles with brass or alloy mounts could be either Dutch or—the later ones—English. The production of opaline in France fell into a decline after the Franco-Prussian war, but lingered on into the 20th century. Examples of English opaline are seen in fig. 96.

Surface Colouring There are three techniques for colouring the surface of glass, and all three were used in the production of scent bottles and cologne flasks: these are overlay, flashing and staining. The overlay technique dates from Roman times and is exemplified by one of glass-making's great achievements, the Portland or Berberini vase (British Museum). It is an elegant urn-shaped vessel in very dark blue glass cased with a thin layer of opaque white. Cutting subsequent to the overlay process produced a decoration of classical figures in bold relief against the blue background.

The technique which produced such a masterpiece was, however, unknown to craftsmen in the centuries that followed until it was redeveloped by Bohemian glass-makers shortly after 1810. It is doubtful whether there is any relationship at all between the Roman and the Bohemian products, although historians are inclined to look favourably on theories indicating links with past achievements. The style of decoration of Bohemian cased glass is hardly ever executed in relief, and rarely figurative in character. It should be mentioned that fine overlaid glass had been made in China as well, and that this was the inspiration for some European work of the late 19th century (see later section on *Art Nouveau*). The production of overlay glass requires not only highly skilled craftsmen but also a good measure of technological experience. The annealing process is complicated by complex stress factors caused by the layering, and the metallic oxides affecting the colouring of individual layers react differently at various temperatures from time to time.

The production of real overlay glass is made possible by the so-called funnel-method, but space does not permit a detailed explanation. Earlier specimens were made of two or three layers but later, after the technique had been introduced into England at the time of the abolition of the excise duty on glass in 1845, fine pieces were made, consisting of up to five layers. The subsequent cutting in deep relief down to the clear glass, revealing the intervening layers, produced most beautiful effects. A quaint but elaborate piece is the boot-shaped bottle already mentioned, in pl. IXa. The precision of these pieces with perfectly symmetrical patterns (figs. 98, 102) must have taxed the craftsman's skill to its limits. The optical effects, magnifying or reducing, which are displayed by scent bottles cut in symmetrical facets are quite extraordinary. Pieces produced by the overlay technique are rather heavy and, unless the shape has been carefully chosen, they appear clumsy. Their thickness, though often unpleasing in decanters or beakers, is no detriment in the case of scent bottles and, even less so, in smelling bottles, since thick glass has a low heat conductivity.

The simplest and cheapest method of producing surface colouring is known as flashing; this consists of dipping the bulb of clear glass at the end of the blow-iron into molten coloured glass, called the pot metal, and then withdrawing it quickly. The bulb is then reheated and formed into the required

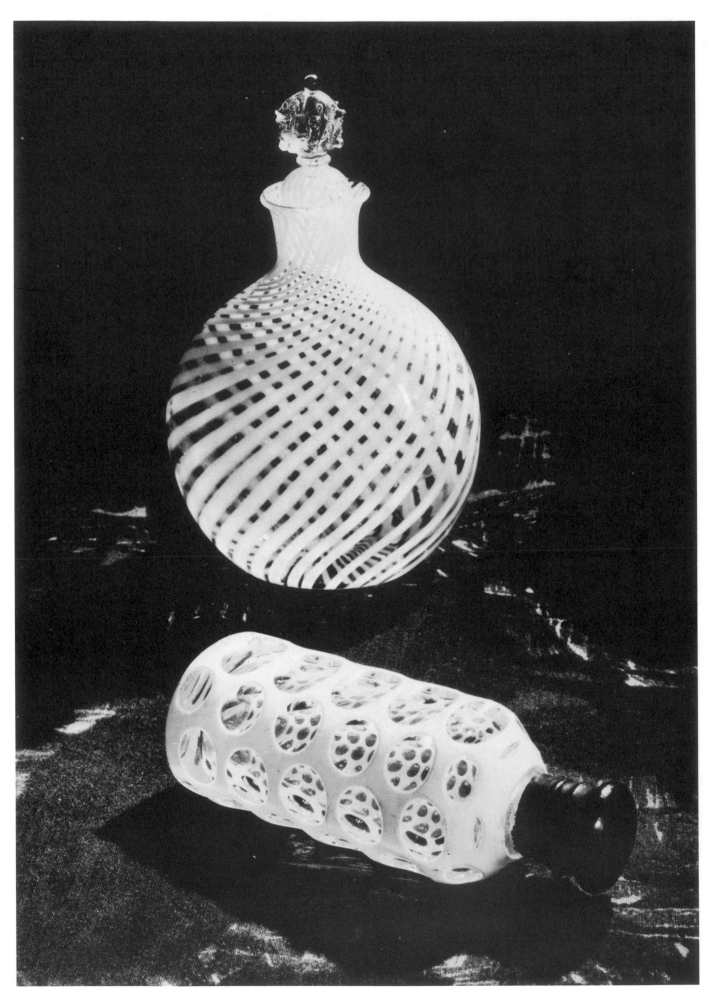

shape by the gaffer. The resulting coloured surface layer is rather thin and does not easily allow for cutting, but wheel-engraved decoration, on account of its shallower nature, may be carried out and is sometimes quite attractive (pl. VI, fig. 103).

A large number of Bohemian glasses were coloured by yet another cheap method, namely staining. This is the technique already used in mediaeval church windows. One of the oldest methods is staining with silver chloride, resulting in a beautiful yellow which is the dominant colour in 14th-century window glass. After 1815 Friedrich Egermann experimented successfully with staining methods, his two main colours being yellow (around 1820) and ruby (probably after 1830). Other glass-houses followed suit and during the next decades a profusion of stained glassware, including scent bottles, was produced. To the colour palette were soon added green, blue, pink and amethyst. Many of these glasses were further embellished by cutting, engraving or gilding. Stained glass scent bottles—and this applies to all other ware—show a greater degree of wear than true overlay pieces on account of the thinness of the stain, and in cut specimens particularly, since the staining tends to come off along the cut edges. When both the interior and exterior surface of a vessel are stained—rarely observed in scent bottles—some experience is needed to distinguish it from real coloured glass. English stained glass was produced after 1850.

Other Colour Embellishments Three more elements in the dazzling multitude of coloured glass made during the late 18th and first half of the 19th century should be considered: *latticino*, *millefiori*, and aventurine glass, all of which have a long ancestry. The *latticino* technique was one of the characteristic innovations of 16th-century Venetian glass-makers. The term is generally applied to glass vessels with insertions of white glass threads (Italian *latte* = milk). Canes of white glass are embedded, usually in clear glass, and manipulated during blowing in such a way that either simple parallel streaks evolve or more complicated interlacing patterns. Venetian glass-houses referred to the products of this technique as *vetro di trina* or *vetro a reticelli*. The latter, also known as lace glass, displays the most intricate patterns. By sucking air out of a bubble of ordinary *latticino* glass the craftsman collapses one half of it into the other, in this way creating a double-walled vessel in which the white glass threads run criss-cross. Glass with white or coloured trailings fused into the surface, as seen in the 19th-century Murano flacon in fig. 102, is similar in appearance but is not true *latticino*. The same technique was employed in some 19th-century English glasses attributed to Nailsea (fig. 87).

Latticino glass was also made outside Venice in an increasingly degenerate form by German glass-houses during the ensuing centuries until glass-makers of the Biedermeier period (encouraged by the offer of a prize for a higher quality of *latticino* glass from the '*Verein zur Beförderung des Gewerbefleisses in Preussen*') interested themselves in the technique. Instead of merely imitating Venetian models, they assimilated *latticino* into their own repertoire of designs; moreover, they did not restrict themselves to white-thread *latticino* work. *Netzgläser*, as they were termed, were produced mainly in the glass-houses of Count Schaffgotsch in Schreiberau (Josephinenhütte), in the glass-house of Neuwelt and in Joachimstal and Schwarzau.

Superb *lattincino* glass, almost exclusively coloured, was made earlier in the first half of the 19th century in France, notably at Choisy-le-Roi and Clichy. Scent bottles produced at the Clichy glass-house are distinguished from Bohemian work of the period by an alternation of coloured stripes which are in some cases ingeniously guided into a zig-zag pattern.

The *millefiori* technique (Italian *mille* = thousand, *fiore* = flower) is another technique dating from Roman times. Its production demands great skill. Canes

opposite page
Fig. 102. *front* Octagonal scent bottle in clear glass with white overlay; the circular cutting, on account of its concavity, achieves an optical effect. Bohemian, 1st half of 19th century. 90 mm high. *back* Purse-shaped flask in clear glass trailed with opaque white glass threads; crown-shaped glass stopper. Venetian (Murano), 19th century. 120 mm high. *DROM-Schatzkammer*

Fig. 103. Icicle-shaped cologne bottle in clear glass overlaid with red and ingeniously cut to form a spiral ribbon; the intervening surface wheel-engraved with flower motifs. Bohemian, 1st half of 19th century. 250 mm high. *Schwarzkopf, Hamburg*

of coloured glass are arranged in the desired pattern, fused together and drawn out into one long cane. The resulting rod is cut into slices and these placed side by side and embedded in clear glass. In this way bowls were made and then finished by grinding and polishing; they are often referred to as *vasa murrhina*. German glass-makers revived the technique during the first half of the 19th century (a group of pieces was shown at an exhibition in Mainz in 1842), but their experiments began in the late 18th century. As far as I know no scent bottles were made using this technique, and for examples we must turn to Italy where a variety of bottles were made by the firm of Franchini and Sons of Venice (fig. 104).

The frequent appearance of these fanciful flacons on the market is an indication of their popularity at the time. They were undoubtedly an integral part of the 19th-century tourist trade in Venice. This applies even more to the small trifles in fig. 105 which were made towards the end of the century. The greatest revival of *millefiori* glass is exemplified by the French paperweights which were traded in the stationery shops of the 19th century for shillings, and which now change hands for hundreds and even thousands of pounds in a senselessly inflated market. In the present context they are of interest only because they were the inspiration of certain English-made inkwells and scent bottles. In no instance can the *millefiori* glass produced over the last hundred and fifty years be compared favourably with its ancient forebears: some indeed is simply vulgar.

In all types of coloured glass discussed so far the colouring substance is completely dissolved in the glass. There are instances, however, in which tiny solid metallic fragments are suspended within the glass. This is the case in the so-called aventurine glass. It received its name through its similarity to aventurine, a hardstone composed of quartz with mica inclusions lending it a golden glitter. The genuine stone has itself been used by craftsmen and

Fig. 104. *Millefiori* bottles. The lower one on the left is probably English (Stourbridge), and the others, with insets of human faces, are Italian. 65 mm, 55 mm and 62 mm high. *J.M., London*

Pl. XVII. Scent bottle with chain and bracelet, enamelled in *basse-taille* technique. 1st half of 19th century. 102 mm high (suspended). *Sotheby & Co. (reproduced by kind permission of H. Ricketts)*

Pl. XVIII. Scent flacon in serpentine; gold cagework with enamelled flowers. English or Dutch, *c.*1835. 64 mm high. *Wartski, London (reproduced by kind permission of H. Ricketts)*

Fig. 105. Collection of perfume phials made for the tourist trade, in variously coloured opaque glass, some streaked or marbled and with inclusions of aventurine glass, some decorated with enamelled flowers. The one on the right of the top row has an inscription in trailed aventurine glass-thread, 'Riccordo Venezia'. Venetian, late 19th century. *J.M., London*

Fig. 106. *left* Scent bottle in speckled reddish glass with incorporated metallic flecks. English (Stourbridge?), late 19th century. 80 mm high. *centre* Art deco perfume bottle in brick-red glass with black glass stopper. French, 1st half of 20th century. 55 mm high. *right* Manufactured glass perfume bottle of a flattened triangular shape, acid-etched and partly polished; brass mount and stopper. Czechoslovakian, *c.*1925. 75 mm high. *J.M., London*

97

jewellers for various purposes; the smelling bottle in pl. II illustrates the point. The first to simulate this rather costly material in glass were the 18th-century Venetian glass-makers. It remains debatable whether they actually set out to do this or whether the discovery came about by accident. Aventurine glass consists of clear or coloured glass with fine fragments of copper mixed with it. German glass-houses, with the help of the celebrated Munich chemist Max Pettenkofer, succeeded in discovering the closely-guarded Venetian secret. They put it to use on a commercial scale for the making of glass beads. In the production of fine Bohemian glass, if one discounts a few instances, it did not play any role worthy of note. I have not seen a scent bottle completely made of aventurine glass but there are numerous examples of early 18th-century bottles containing streaks of aventurine glass (see pl. IVb). In 19th-century Venice speckled glass was made in various glass-houses. Examples of aventurine inclusions are seen in the scent bottles illustrated in figs. 105 and 106.

Lithyalin Bottles Purists among connoisseurs of glass will reject out of hand any attempt to imitate other materials in this medium. There are indeed, some lovers of fine glass to whom plain drinking vessels in English 18th-century lead glass are the ultimate in glass-making. In their eye the introduction of air twists or opaque twist stems was a mere caprice which detracted rather than contributed to the pristine beauty of the free-blown glass. Was the miraculously clear material, by definition neither liquid nor solid, not enough in itself? Barrington Haynes refers to decoration on glass as 'gilding the lily'. When considering Friedrich Egermann's lithyalin glass, a glass which seeks to pass for semi-precious stone and which represents the finest achievement in the making of 'stone glass', one has to bear in mind that over the centuries glass and stone have often been rivals in the field of the applied arts, and this is lithyalin's *raison d'être*. The gilding-the-lily argument simply does not apply.

Long before Egermann's time (1777–1864), in fact from the beginning of the 16th century, Venetian glass-houses had succeeded in producing mottled or marbled glass by allowing quantities of glass of different colours to mingle while still liquid. In this way they produced their famous *Schmelzglas* made in imitation of agate, chalcedony, onyx and aventurine. (The German term for this type of glass, from *schmelzen* = to melt, is now generally used, but one also finds it referred to as agate-glass or *calcedonio*, by which term is was known to the Venetians themselves.) A similar product made during the 17th century in Venice is known as *Karneolglas*, and this is characterized by reddish veins. No *Schmelzglas* scent bottle seems to be known.

Friedrich Egermann, born in Schlucknau, was the most original and successful of the Bohemian glass-makers of the Empire and Biedermeier period. The life story of this basically self-taught man makes fascinating reading. The most outstanding among his numerous innovations in the field of glass technology, and the most laudable artistically, is his *Edelsteinglas* (*Edelstein* = precious stone) which at the suggestion of Viennese friends he called lithyalin (Greek *lithos* = stone). It was patented in 1828 and surprisingly large quantities of highly accomplished pieces appeared on the market in 1829. Experiments for its production must have begun years earlier, for in 1824 Egermann made mention in a written contract of previous '*mineralischen Farbversuchen*' (experiments with mineral colours).

The peculiar patterns in lithyalin were achieved by the introduction of minerals into the mixture of differently coloured glass masses. In order to confuse his rivals Egermann labelled his new product as '*Edelsteinglas aus vegetablischen Stoffen*' (precious-stone glass made from vegetable substances), thus creating the myth that he used concoctions of ashes of exotic plants for the colouring of his wares. What distinguishes the best of his lithyalin from all previous attempts of this kind is the regular, often symmetrical, arrangement

Fig. 107. Group of lithyalin bottles and a vinaigrette (*front*) by Friedrich Egermann. Bohemian, 2nd quarter of 19th century. 68 mm, 62 mm and 70 mm high. *J.M.*, *London* (vinaigrette *Leslie Scott*)

of the 'grain' of the piece; in most instances the streaky pattern is further emphasized by a cutting technique of high precision. The overall colours of individual pieces range from leek green and olive green to bluish-mauve and various shades of red, the most common resembling the colour of sealing wax (pl. IXb and c). The beautifully polished surface is most remarkable in all Egermann lithyalin glass, and this is one of the features which distinguish it from rival products.

The imitation of one's work is the best compliment, and this glass was copied by various makers in Silesia, Bohemia and Bavaria, and later in France. One might even suggest that here is the paternity of some English pressed glass. But no one came near to achieving the quality of glass made by the great master.

The swamping of the market by the rather coarse products of his competitors and the enormous production costs of high-quality lithyalin may account for the fact that it was only produced over a period of about twelve years. It must also be pointed out that similar aesthetic effects could be achieved much more cheaply by ceramic processes.

The beauty of Egermann's lithyalin is revealed to its full extent in larger pieces such as beakers, goblets, toilet water flasks and vases. Sometimes these are further embellished by gilding (monograms, insect or flower motifs, formal borders and, more rarely, portraits). Earlier examples are rather transparent, whereas the later pieces are thick-walled and almost always elaborately cut. Scent bottles in this glass (figs. 107, 108, pl. IXb and c) are extremely rare and almost always in reddish colours.

Hyalith Bottles Unlike *Schmelzglas*, black opaque glass has no ancestor in history. It was invented around 1817 in the Georgenthal factory of Egermann's compatriot Georg Franz August Longueval, Count Buquoy (1781–1851). This versatile nobleman, who also owned several other glass-houses in this area where glass-making had been thriving since the 16th century, made a name for himself with numerous inventions, the foremost of which was his process of making a brick-red glass and, jointly with one of his directors, Bartholomäus Rössler, black hyalith.

Fig. 108. Perfume flask in lithyalin glass (reddish-brown) by Friedrich Egermann; silver mount and top. Bohemian, 2nd quarter of 18th century. 120 mm high. *R.*, *Frankfurt-Main*

99

Fig. 109. Small flacon in hyalith glass with gilt decoration, suspended from a finger-ring. Bohemian, c.1850. 50 mm high. *J.M.*, *London*

It cannot definitely be stated that Count Buquoy invented his hyalith solely to produce wares in imitation of Wedgwood's basalt ware, but quite clearly the immense popularity of the latter's innovation furthered the sale of hyalith and also influenced it artistically. Adaptations of Wedgwood motifs and patterns in gold or silver frequently appear on pieces made in Georgenthal. In contrast to Egermann's lithyalin, the shiny deep-black surface of hyalith makes it an ideal vehicle for gilding. Apart from classical motifs, chinoiseries are most prominently represented, but there are also all the decorative elements mentioned for lithyalin. The extent to which the rage for Wedgwood ware influenced the mind of these Bohemian glass artists is demonstrated by certain pieces —shaped and decorated in Wedgwood fashion—in which the entire surface has been made matt to give the appearance of basalt ware.

Most of these items were produced with enormous skill and at great cost which could have been made much more easily and cheaply in a ceramic medium.[18] Scent bottles to be carried in a reticule, made of hyalith, are rare (fig. 109), but in a private collection there is a small pear-shaped standing bottle about 70 mm. high. There are many hyalith scent and toilet-water flasks for the dressing table. The most common among them are thick-walled, square or rectangular flacons, the squat shape of which gives them the secondary function of a paper weight. The perfume burner illustrated in fig. 48 is particularly interesting on account of its unusual shape. Since no signed pieces of hyalith are known, and this applies equally to Egermann's lithyalin, the attribution of this piece to Buquoy is open to question. As can be expected, Count Buquoy did not long remain alone in the field, but none of his contemporary or later rivals ever achieved the same success. Perhaps one should mention that, independent of Buquoy, black glass was invented by chance in the glass-house of Zechlin (Prussia) in the first decade of the 19th century; the glass made there never became a serious competitor to that of Georgenthal and scent bottles were not in their range of products.

VICTORIAN BOTTLES

Cameo Glass Bottles The technique of casing glass, as mentioned earlier, had been successfully practised in Roman times. The greatest achievement in this field, the celebrated Portland Vase, inspired John Northwood (1837–1902) to produce his cameo glass. In 1876, after three years of solid work, he completed his replica of the famous original housed in the British Museum. The full story of the revival of cameo technique (that is, cutting in relief) on cased glass has been narrated by G. Beard.[19] The reader should not confuse the term cameo glass with *crystallo ceramie* mentioned earlier (glass with cameo incrustations).

The two firms mainly involved were Richardson of Wordsley and Thomas Webb and Sons of Stourbridge. It was the latter firm in which the most important followers of Northwood, namely the Woodall brothers, George and Thomas and the Pearces, father and son, were employed. Scent bottles feature prominently in the quantity of cameo glass produced at Stourbridge. Since few are signed, one cannot ascertain who was actually responsible for their making. The commonest type of cameo scent bottle is the one illustrated in pl. IXe. Bottles of this shape are always decorated with plant motifs, the most frequent being a representation of the maidenhair fern. The basic colours range from blue, green, and yellow-green to a shade of yellow; pink and red tones are rarer. The cherry motif in the illustration is also found on a vase (Union Museum, New York) allegedly made by J. T. Fereday at Thomas Webb and Sons. Whether the same craftsman was responsible for the scent bottle shown here, or indeed all bottles of this type, is open to conjecture. When studying a number of these bottles one cannot help feeling that they lack the artistic *élan* lavished

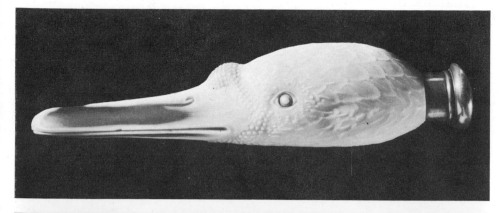

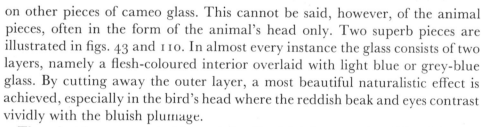

Fig. 110. Cameo glass scent bottle in the shape of a duck's head. English (Thomas Webb and Sons), late 19th century. Approx. 110 mm long. *Leslie Scott*

Fig. 111. Cameo glass scent bottle in the shape of an owl's head; red ground overlaid in white and carved to reveal red eyes and beak. English (Daniel and Lionel Pearce). 65 mm high. *Christie, Manson & Woods Ltd.*

Fig. 112. *left* Scent bottle of a flattened tear shape in clear glass, engraved on the wheel on both sides with bird and flower motifs; unmounted. 65 mm high. *right* Circular scent bottle, perhaps inspired by an ammonite, in leek-green glass with brownish enamel paint; unmounted. 40 mm high. English (Daniel and Lionel Pearce), late 19th century. *J.M., London*

on other pieces of cameo glass. This cannot be said, however, of the animal pieces, often in the form of the animal's head only. Two superb pieces are illustrated in figs. 43 and 110. In almost every instance the glass consists of two layers, namely a flesh-coloured interior overlaid with light blue or grey-blue glass. By cutting away the outer layer, a most beautiful naturalistic effect is achieved, especially in the bird's head where the reddish beak and eyes contrast vividly with the bluish plumage.

These bottles were probably made by Daniel (1817–1907) or Lionel (1852–1926) Pearce. G. Beard records[20] that there exists a pattern book by Daniel Pearce in which there are sketches of, among other items, twenty-five scent bottles, one of them in the shape of an owl's head (for the actual piece see fig. 111). In style and technique this beautiful bottle is similar to those mentioned above.

The Pearces did not work solely in cased glass, they also produced pieces which were cut and engraved with great skill. Their versatility is demonstrated by a number of scent bottles which Lionel Pearce kept in his private collection and which came on to the market a few years ago (figs. 42, 112–14). None of them was mounted and one must assume that most of them are unique. The realistic representation of a crocodile's head, in fig. 114, is not made in overlay glass but cut in such a way that when held against the light the creature's teeth become ferociously apparent. The aesthetic value of this bottle as a perfume container is, it must be said, open to question. Certainly no delicate member of the female sex would want to carry in her reticule a bottle the net weight of which, unmounted, is almost six ounces.

Whereas Northwood and most other makers of cameo glass were inspired by Roman glass, the Pearces drew their inspiration from Chinese snuff bottles, as did, indeed, many of their contemporaries, the creators of *art nouveau* glass.

Fig. 113. Group of scent bottles made by Daniel and Lionel Pearce. *left* Cameo glass scent bottle, opaque ground decorated in a carved red overlay; facing side has the words 'Dear May' set in a circular depression surrounded by clouds, and the reverse a house in a landscape and an oil lamp. Modern silver mount by Miss Dorothy Pearce. 75 mm high. *centre* Cameo glass scent bottle formed as a dahlia, yellow ground with white overlay petals and curling stalk on one side. 60 mm high. *right* Enamel cased cameo of glass scent bottle; facing side has two ducks (emblematic of marital bliss) swimming, and the reverse birds in flight over a moor. 65 mm high. *Christie, Manson & Woods Ltd.*

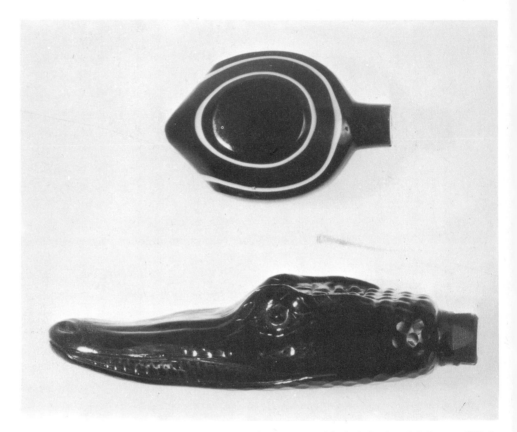

Fig. 114. *above* Tear-shaped overlay glass scent bottle in imitation of striated agate. 65 mm high. *below* Dark reddish-brown glass scent bottle shaped as an alligator's head. 120 mm long. English (Daniel and Lionel Pearce), late 19th century. *J.M., London*

When the Pearce collection came up for sale at Christie's (2nd May 1966) it contained several lots of Chinese bottles on which they had modelled their own.

Double Scent Bottles Perhaps there is no other type of scent bottle in history which has surpassed, in sheer quantity and variety of detail, the English double scent bottle. Strictly a Victorian invention, it has no ancestor and nothing of its kind follows after it. We do not know who conceived the idea of combining the scent bottle with the smelling bottle or the vinaigrette but we are aware that both existed independently in the first half of the 19th century, and were an essential part of the contents of the lady's reticule. The combined container did not appear on the scene until after 1850.

Double scents are made in great variety and in every conceivable material. They all have the same basic design (figs. 63, 115): two cylindrical or prismatic bottles (usually of equal length) are fused together at their bases to form a two-compartment container, one compartment holding smelling salts—in some instances it is a vinaigrette, in which case it is smaller—and the other liquid

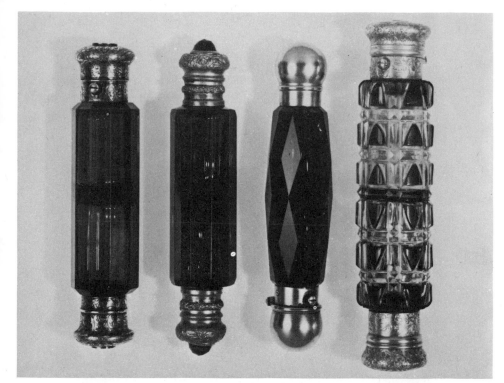

Fig. 115. Group of double scent bottles. *left to right* Ruby glass with scroll-engraved silver caps; two deep blue glass bottles, one superbly cut and polished, the other with blue glass 'diamonds' mounted in the caps; deeply cut light blue overlay on clear glass. English, 2nd half of 19th century. 120 mm, 125 mm, 120 mm and 140 mm high. *J.M., London*

Fig. 116. Group of fancy silver bottles. *left to right* Cone-shaped, Birmingham (H. & H.), 1902; unmarked bottle with shell-motif, German (?), *c.*1890, 40 mm high; bottle with rouge compartment under hinged lid, enamelled flower decoration and engraved owner's initials (on reverse), Birmingham, 1888, 68 mm high; double scent bottle in the shape of a Christmas cracker with enamel panel, London (S. Mordan), 1883, 102 mm long. *below* Horn-shaped double scent bottle, London (S. Mordan), 1872, 109 mm long.

perfume or cologne. The perfume compartment is usually closed by a metal screw cap (sometimes with a ground glass stopper underneath), whereas the smelling salts compartment has a specially designed hinged lid fitted with a spring which springs open when the release button is pressed. The latter is a most ingenious device to stop the evaporation of the volatile substances. The metal cap contains a glass disc which is pressed against the plain ground top surface of the bottle by a metal spring. This explains why the cap springs open when the release button is touched only gently. So effective is the closure achieved by this method that the contents of bottles which have not been touched since Victorian times still retain their pungent properties.

Though these bottles were produced in a number of materials, the great majority were in glass. A double scent bottle in silver, glass-lined and resembling a Christmas cracker, is depicted in fig. 116; sometimes one finds bottles with decorative engraving in less expensive nickel alloy and a few engine-turned metal basket-work, again glass-lined. Bottles within a silver-gilt cage, of the type illustrated in fig. 63, are extremely fine. As for double scent bottles in porcelain, these are relatively rare.

The glass bottles are usually made separately but fused together in such a way that the dividing line can hardly be seen. The most primitive types are of moulded glass and usually decorated with a crude hobnail pattern (fig. 63). This type is mounted with gun-metal screw caps and without spring lid. The most common glass bottles, however, are octagonal in cross-section with flat panels. Completely cylindrical bottles, which are usually elaborately cut, are rare. Uncut bottles in clear glass are also rare; in these the interior surface of the smelling salt compartment is in most cases so corroded that the entire bottle looks rather unsightly. Most glass double scents are coloured, ruby red being the most popular colour, followed by blue and green; bottles in ópaline or uranium green or yellow are relatively rare. I have seen double scent bottles which were amber in colour and also deep purple manganese specimens. Bottles in which the two halves are of different colours are as rare as they are hideous. Thick-walled glass bottles display most of the cut patterns typical of their period and one finds a fair number of double scent bottles in overlay glass (fig. 115)—the cheaper versions in flashed glass.

Double scent bottles with engraved or gilt decorated panels are quite exceptional; these are normally made of opaline or milk glass, and sometimes their shape deviates from the basic design of a double scent bottle. The bottle in the form of a cross (fig. 117) is unique in combining four containers in one. The hinged specimen in the same illustration is not uncommon; I have recently seen a piece of this sort disguised as a set of opera glasses contained in a special leather case. In some types the central metal mount forms a locket to hold a photograph or bears an engraved monogram; one of the caps will also often bear a monogram. One also finds hinged bottles with a vinaigrette inserted into the base of one of the pair, thus making it a triple bottle. In cases where a scent bottle is joined with a vinaigrette, the part containing the latter is usually much smaller than the perfume compartment (figs. 88, 89). In most cases twin bottles of this combination differ in shape from the typical double scent bottle, but in the few instances where this shape has been adopted the combined bottle, on account of its asymmetry, looks rather unbalanced. To overcome this aesthetic problem, makers of scent bottles have resorted to all sorts of shapes, some of which border on the absurd. Eric Delieb illustrates a perfume flask in the shape of a champagne bottle—the top quite convincingly taking the form of a foiled cork—with the small vinaigrette inserted into the base. In the same book there is a picture of a silver twin bottle made by Th. Johnson of London in 1873 in the form of a cannon barrel.[21]

The most elegant and certainly the most appropriate solution was the twin bottle in the shape of a horn. This little trifle must have been extremely popular, judging by the many pieces that have survived. Horn-shaped twin bottles (fig. 116) were made in both glass and silver and were small enough to be worn on a chatelaine.

The makers of double scent bottles catered for a wide market, from the simple to the sophisticated, from the poor to the extravagant. This is reflected in the great variety of glass—from plain coloured glass to beautifully wheel-cut flint-glass—and even more so in the range of metal mounts used.

In the simplest examples, usually the earlier ones, the caps at each end are screw-attached and often directly screwed on to the glass. The leak-proof fastening is achieved by a cork disc inside the cap. More elaborate specimens have screw mounts cemented on the glass on one side and a one or three lugger-hinged lid on the other. The material ranges from brass to silver and gold; electro-deposit gilded brass alloy is the most common. The caps are plain or engraved, or embossed in high relief, and sometimes their flattened tops bear a cartouche with the owner's initials or a motto engraved on it. The bottle with silver-gilt mounts and inset coral 'gems' in fig. 63 is obviously rather expensive; in a less extravagant specimen (fig. 115) the alloy caps have a cut-glass 'jewel'

Fig. 117. Selection of fancy bottles, all in ruby red glass. *above l. to r.* Smelling bottle cum whistle, silver mounts without hall-marks, English, *c.*1880, 86 mm high; cross-shaped bottle with four compartments, silver repoussé screw-top, suspensory ring and central mount with owner's initials, English, registration mark (on reverse) for 1865, 109 mm high; cylindrical smelling bottle with glass stopper beneath screw-top, hall-mark CM, Birmingham, 1900, 75 mm high. *below* Hinged double scent bottle, without hall-mark, English, *c.*1885 (one often finds double scent bottles of this kind made in imitation of opera glasses), 136 mm long.

inserted into the centre which matches the blue glass of the bottle. Finer bottles were traded in a specially-made leather case, with the name of the retailer on the lining of the lid. Makers' names and patent numbers are often found engraved around the centre beneath the glass disc inside the hinged cap. Among them the firm of Samuel Mordan features prominently. These names in conjunction with hall-marks indicate that the two centres of manufacture for double scent bottles were London and Birmingham.

The vogue for double scent bottles began in the middle of the 19th century—the earliest known hall-marked specimen is dated 1851—and continued into the last decade. Thus earlier examples qualify as antiques. On the whole they represent an interesting period of scent history. Most of them were mass produced and made by mechanical or semi-mechanical means. Some of them, and certain single-compartment scent or toilet water bottles, came from ladies' travelling bags, or vanity cases as they would be called today. Magazines of the late 19th century contain illustrated advertisements of these, offered for sale by firms dealing in jewellery and luxury articles which are still in business in the more expensive shopping areas of London today. Remnants of these long discarded bags abound in antique shops. Often several bottles of the same pattern but different dimensions have stayed together and are offered as a set.

The Vinaigrette The vinaigrette, though usually made of metal, is included in this section because of its association with Victorian glass bottles. Of all containers used in the history of perfumery the vinaigrette proved to be the most short-lived. It came into existence during the closing years of the 18th century, had its heyday in the early Victorian era and suffered an almost sudden decline as it entered the second half of the 19th century. It has been stated that it represents a later development of the pomander, but this is not quite true. The pomander is an open vessel, whereas the vinaigrette has to be as tightly closed as possible to prevent the evaporation of its contents. Any apertures it had were exposed only momentarily to permit the inhalation of the invigorating or even restorative vapours of its contents. Since the vinaigrette is basically a box and belongs rather to the snuff box and *bonbonnière* family, only brief treatment is called for in this context. A sufficiently exhaustive description of 19th-century vinaigrettes is to be found in the works of Eric Delieb[22] and Therle Hughes.[23]

In brief, the vinaigrette is a small but usually elaborately ornamented container for holding various aromatic substances, including camphor, dissolved in strong vinegar. Small pieces of Turkish sponge contained beneath a perforated disc or grid hold the liquid, and the whole container is tightly sealed by either a hinged or a screwed-on metal lid. As a precaution against corrosion the interior of the box and the grid, if not made of silver or gold, is heavily silvered.

This basic construction goes back to the so-called pouncet-box of Elizabethan times. This was a flattened box, usually circular, with a pierced lid; it is related to the pomander. Another version, already closer in construction to the 19th-century vinaigrette, was the essence box. It was a shallower box, round or rectangular, with a lift-off lid. Beneath a metal grill was a solid mixture of rice-starch, pulverized orris root and magnesium carbonate. The resulting smell was much more pleasing but less effective than the rather pungent vinegar of its predecessor. Most vinaigrettes were made in metal but in Victorian times the body in quite a number of cases was made of glass or even porcelain. The fore-runners of vinaigrettes were also built into the handles of walking sticks. Sir Charles Jackson, in his *Illustrated History of English Plate* (1911), depicts a 'physician's walking-stick' with a perforated handle, dated about 1613.

As indicated above, the main active ingredient used in a vinaigrette is vinegar or, to be more precise, acetic acid. The admixture of essential oils does not inhibit its pungency but makes it a more agreeable and balanced odour. There are many recipes, which can be distinguished according to the dominant note: *vinaigre à la rose, vinaigre à la violette, vinaigre de Cologne*, etc. The legendary *Vinaigre des Quatre Voleurs* or, to use the chemist's terminology, *acetum quattuor latronum*, is famous. The story behind this name runs as follows: in Marseilles at the time of the plague there were four villains who, under the pretence of succouring the sick, indulged in body-snatching, though they themselves, strangely enough, did not contract the disease. When apprehended, one of them saved his neck by revealing the recipe of the prophylactic they had apparently used. According to Septimus Piesse[24] it consisted of certain quantities of common wormwood, Roman wormwood, rosemary, sage, mint, rue, lavender flowers, garlic, calamus, cinnamon, cloves, nutmeg, camphor, alcohol or brandy and strong vinegar.

'Victoriana' It is rather unfortunate that certain periods or styles are referred to by the name of the reigning monarch of the time. Not only is this practice crude from the point of view of dating, but it is unjustified, giving a false impression as to the monarch's personal association with the style. Only a few sovereigns, such as Louis XIV, Louis XV and George IV, really influenced artistic movements of their period, or actively furthered them.

Likewise, a monarch cannot be blamed for a dearth of artistic creativity or originality, or for thriving bad taste during his or her reign, since such phenomena are governed by forces beyond his or her control. Queen Victoria would certainly not be amused to see the mountains of rubbish on sale in upgraded junk shops and antique supermarkets which is described as 'Victoriana', but which the connoisseur will not touch. Nevertheless all these monstrosities reflect the taste of an age. In many instances they appeal to us emotionally—'Grandma had one of them'—rather than artistically.

The industrial revolution made it possible to produce by the thousand items which were previously hand-made and the steady rise in the standard of living of the middle and working classes led to an increasing demand for certain luxuries which had hitherto been the preserve of the wealthy. Victorian scent bottles outnumber the sum total of all scent bottles made during the preceding four centuries. Naturally enough, design was geared to the artistic demands and financial means of the new customers, who required imitations of contemporary objects made in precious materials or anachronistic pieces based on objects of earlier periods. It was an eclectic period indeed. There was hardly any earlier style which was not imitated or 'improved' upon. One need only compare the clumsy, machine-made metal openwork and the top caps applied to flacons seen in figs. 99 and 118 with the superb work of the 18th century (figs. 78–80) to note the decline in craftsmanship and taste, a decline by no means confined to England at that time. Imperial vanity and affluence had its counterpart in Germany with the *Gründerzeit* ('foundation period'), beginning after the conclusion of the Franco-Prussian war (1871) when there was an influx of vast amounts of capital into the country.

I must stress that here we are dealing with Victoriana, with what the term implies today, and not the good or at least passable Victorian scent and smelling bottles discussed above. We must also remember the many contemporary critics who voiced their dissent, foremost among them John Ruskin and

Fig. 118. Assembly of fancy bottles, the ones in the top row made of glass harnessed with machine-made open metalwork. *below l.* China bottle in the shape of an acorn; *below r.* china bottle in the shape of a sea-shell, with a silver mount marked S. Mordan, London 1885. English, late 19th century.

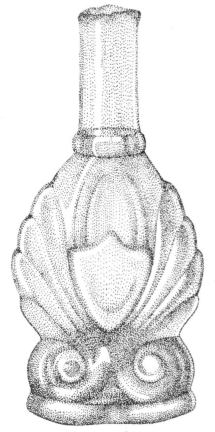

120. Drawing of an early manufactured scent bottle of the type seen in
fig. 119, unearthed from a Victorian
rubbish tip. English. 80 mm high.
J.M., London

William Morris. In addition, to be just to the manufacturers of the criticized
merchandise, of which only a representative selection is illustrated here—the
material available is inexhaustible and defies classification—it must be said
that they were not working with posterity in mind. They satisfied the require-
ments of the day and, in a way, initiated a trend which finally led to the
throwaway goods of our time (figs. 119, 120). Who could have foreseen that
objects once destined for the dustbin would be sought after and traded at
ridiculously high prices in the bric-à-brac market of the space age? Moreover,
a glance at today's souvenir shops and even the gift departments of elegant
department stores makes the critic of the past painfully aware that he should
not complain about past lapses of taste. The illustrations speak for themselves
(figs. 66, 90–92, 106, 121–132).

There are scent bottles in all sorts of shapes; animals, guns, pistols, champagne bottles, shells and so on. In the *Lady's Pictorial* of 1888, Messrs. Drew of
156 Leadenhall Street, prolific makers of scent bottles, advertised a 'lucky
horseshoe scent bottle' as an idea for Christmas gifts, and the same firm,
together with Liberty's, also offered chatelaines with scent bottles attached, the
latter being based on antique Dutch and Flemish designs. Travelling cases
with sets of scent and smelling bottles were also available in profusion. One case
had three conical scent bottles 'so arranged that when the case is opened the
bottles move upwards with a spring'.

The charming and ingenious device in fig. 133 seems to be lost altogether.
No specimen has survived, apparently, but it is described by S. G. W. Piesse in
The Art of Perfumery, as follows: 'As a means of carrying scent about the person,

Fig. 121. Group of china bottles for the not-so-rich, all with brass mounts. *above l.* Bottle with portrait of Richard Wagner; *above r.* pseudo-rococo scene. *centre Eau de Cologne* bottle inscribed (on reverse) 'Johann Maria Farina'. *below* Two bottles depicting stage beauties and a souvenir bottle from Cologne. German, turn of the century.

Fig. 122. Group of china bottles. *above l. to r.* Flattened bottle with Oriental scene, unmarked; cylindrical bottle with blue underglaze decoration (maker's mark on mount D.L., Birmingham 1905); two ivory-coloured flattened Worcester bottles. *below l. to r.* Smelling bottle with landscapes in sepia colours, unmarked, hinged silver repoussé top *c.*1885; two Worcester bottles of flattened circular shape with blue underglaze decoration, one commemorating Queen Victoria's Silver Jubilee (1887), the other displaying the familiar willow pattern (mount by S. Mordan, London 1886); cylindrical bottle in imitation of carved ivory (maker's mark on mount F.S., Birmingham 1889).

Fig. 123. China bottles. *above l. to r.*
Egg-shaped with coloured flowers
on a white ground, silver screw-top,
marked C.W., Birmingham 1892;
Coalport bottle with white flowers
and ivy foliage on a gold ground.
below l. to r. Smelling bottle with
bird and nest motif on a yellow
ground, with silver-gilt mount and
patent spring lid, marked S.M.
(S. Mordan), Birmingham 1893;
unidentified porcelain bottle with
silver-gilt mounts. All English,
approx. 70 mm high.

Fig. 124. *left* Mass-produced bottle
in imitation of 18th-century
porcelain. English, 20th century (?).
90 mm high. *right* Blue opaque glass
bottle with white enamel decoration
in the so-called Mary Gregory style.
English, 2nd half of 19th century.
70 mm high.

Fig. 125. Openwork china bottle. English (Locke & Co.?), late 19th century. 85 mm high.

Fig. 126. China scent bottle of a flattened oval shape with pâte-sur-pâte decoration. French, 2nd half of 19th century. Approx. 90 mm high. *Parfumerie Fragonard, Grasse*

Fig. 127. *above l. to r.* Flacon made of a palm seed; smelling case carved out of ivory; flacon in ebony with silver mount. *below l. to r.* Scent bottle made out of a peach-stone, with ivory stopper; smelling capsule in boxwood; smelling capsule in bronze. Various origins, actual size.

111

Fig. 128. Victorian trifles. The acorn-shaped piece (35 mm high) is a vinaigrette, and the brass-mounted piece (*below r.*) is fitted with mirrors (50 mm high). All English, late 19th century. *J.M., London*

Fig. 129. Scent bottle made of a pair of shells, glued together and harnessed with machine-tooled brass; brass-covered cork stopper. English, 2nd half of 19th century. 75 mm high. *J.M., London*

Fig. 130. Collection of travelling containers for scent bottles, each holding one glass flacon. The one on the right, in finely carved ivory openwork, fits into the one to the left of it (89 mm high). All English, late 19th century.

Pl. XIX. Enamel box in the form of a sedan chair. German (Fromery), mid-18th century. 102 mm high. *Sotheby & Co. (reproduced by kind permission of H. Ricketts)*

Pl. XX. Enamel scent bottle of a flattened pear shape, with painted ornaments and Watteauesque scene; gilt metal mount and foliate stopper. English (South Staffordshire), *c.*1760. 127 mm high. *DROM-Schatzkammer*

Pl. XXII. Enamel combined scent bottle and *bonbonnière* (or smelling box), painted with floral motifs and country scene. English (South Staffordshire), *c.*1765. 103 mm high. *DROM-Schatzkammer*

Pl. XXI. Enamel scent bottle of a flattened pear shape, with painted floral ornaments and scene of a couple drinking; silver mount. German, 2nd quarter 18th century. 80 mm high. *DROM-Schatzkammer*

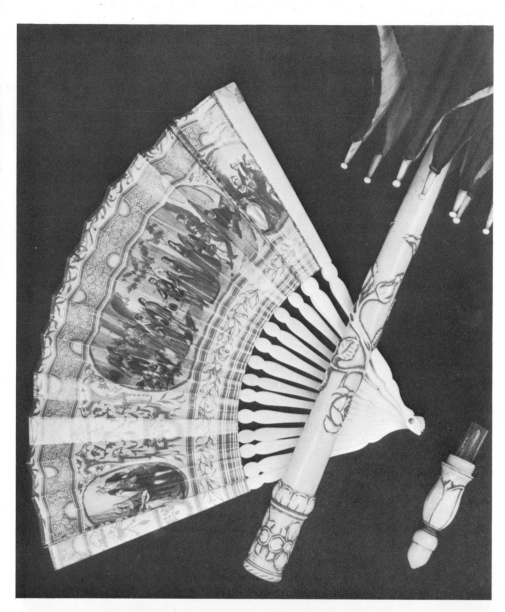

Fig. 131. Handle of a lady's umbrella containing fan and scent bottle; carved ivory. English, 19th century.

Fig. 132. Selection of small perfume or smelling bottles, all but one to be attached to a chain, probably a chatelaine. Mostly English, 19th century. Actual size.

Fig. 133. Fountain finger-ring. 19th century.

Fig. 134. *above l. to r.* Walnut-shaped silver flacon, English (Birmingham?), 1898, 41 mm high; egg-shaped china bottle with a silver screw-top taking the shape of a bird's head, English, *c.*1885, 37 mm high; similar to preceding piece but with silver body, representing a fine example of parts 'married' to deceive (head with London discharge mark, body with Birmingham mark of 1889), 38 mm high. *below l. to r.* Silver bottles with floral ornament; maker S. Mordan, London 1887, 39.5 mm high; maker F.S.P., Birmingham 1901, 28.5 mm high; maker C.M., Birmingham 1889, 41 mm high.

Fig. 135. Selection of silver open-work flacons. *above l. to r.* Clear glass bottle in silver cage, without hall-mark, and silver screw-top with inserted blue glass 'gem', foreign, *c.*1900, 35 mm high; flattened glass bottle in silver filigree cage, Yugoslavian, 1906, 52.4 mm high; smelling bottle in green glass, with glass stopper beneath hinged lid, maker G.E.M., Birmingham 1902, 52 mm high. *below* Silver filigree thimbles containing small cut-glass scent bottles, the screw-top (*left and centre*) containing either tape measure or bobbin. English (?), late 19th century. 50 mm, 20 mm, 48 mm and 25 mm high.

the fountain finger-ring has recently become famous. The delight of all who have seen this little conceit is most gratifying to its inventor. It is at once useful and ornamental. By the least pressure, the wearer of the ring can cause a jet of perfume to arise from it at any time desired—thus every one can carry with him to a ball, concert, or sick chamber, enough scent, so refreshing! for the time being. The practical application of this invention causes a good deal of merriment and laughter. A gentleman who abhors perfume, unless it be snuff, "squeezing" a lady's hand, will receive a shower of the eternal frangipanni or kiss-me-quick, much to the delight of all present at being thus sweetly "found out". The rings can be filled with perfume with the greatest ease—thus: Press the ball at the back of the ring nearly flat, pour scent into a cup and dip the ring into it; the elasticity of the ball will then draw the perfume into the interior till full.'

For people who could not afford silver flacons—and a large number of 19th-century silver bottles are very beautiful, and seldom border on the vulgar —the introduction of the electro-plating process by George Elkington (1801–65) of Birmingham was a god-sent gift. By this method, based on Volta's discovery in 1799, silver was deposited by electrolysis on to an alloy known as German silver. Many of the machine-made chatelaines, mounts and metal embellishments were treated by this novel method, which brought its inventor a greater fortune than many a manufacturer of real silver objects.

The number of china scent bottles produced by English souvenir factories was enormous. Whether any bottles were made by the firm of W. H. Goss and Sons of Stoke-on-Trent, whose wares barely surpass junk-shop level, I do not know; one of the pieces in fig. 139 may come from this factory, but it is not marked. Another bottle in the same material, inappropriately shaped like a teapot and with the emblems of Whitestable, came to light recently in an antique dealer's private chamber of horrors. There is hardly any antique shop in the country without one or several china bottles as seen in figs. 121 and 139. Most of these trifles, which do not lack a certain charm, were made, like so many china souvenirs, by firms in Germany, notably by the Silesian firm of P. Donath and some factories in Bavaria. Representations of English townscapes or personalities (see the bottle depicting Lily Langtry of Victorian music hall fame in fig. 139) or the presence of English excise marks do not necessarily point to English manufacture.

Fig. 136. Selection of variously shaped and decorated silver flacons. *above l. to r.* Unmarked ribbed bottle, German or French, early 20th century, 61 mm high; flacon with owner's name (Lalla), English (Chester), 1891, 41 mm high; bottle probably imported from the Far East, *c.*1920. *centre l. to r.* Silver case to take glass phial, maker C.W., Birmingham 1801, 39 mm high; unmarked bottle with formal foliage motifs, foreign, *c.*1895, 46 mm high; plain smelling bottle with owner's initials engraved, not hall-marked, early 20th century, 57 mm high. *below l. to r.* Bottle in the shape of a pilgrim's flask, maker S. Mordan, London 1873, 52 mm high; slim bottle with central panel to take owner's initials, German, *c.*1900, 70 mm high; bottle heavily decorated with flower motifs, Dutch or German, *c.*1890, 58 mm high.

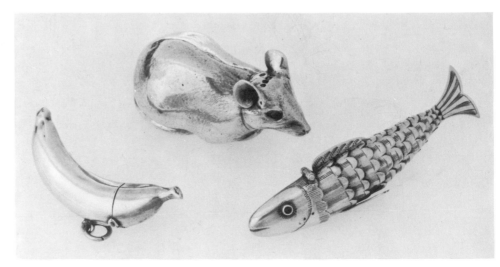

Fig. 137. Silver scent bottles in various shapes: a banana, with silver screw-top beneath hinged lid, Birmingham (L. & S.) 1904, 59 mm long; a mouse, the head forming the screw-top, London (T.S.) 1883, 62 mm long; smelling bottle in the shape of an articulated fish, Dutch or German, 18th century, 80 mm long.

Fig. 138. *left to right* Lantern-shaped smelling bottle, London (S. Mordan) *c.*1880, 81 mm high; ribbed bottle with tight-fitting stopper beneath hinged lid, London (maker's name illegible) 1865, 68 mm high; hexagonal flacon, Birmingham (J.G.) 1931, 76 mm high; heavily decorated smelling bottle, Birmingham (A.W.P.) 1894, 64 mm high.

Fig. 139. China bottles. *above l. to r.* Depicting a Japanese beauty, silver screw-top with Birmingham hall-mark of 1904; portrait of Lily Langtry smelling lilies, silver screw-top with Birmingham hall-mark of 1904; same portrait and date as preceding piece but with maker's mark R.P. *below l.* Brighton souvenir bottle with brass mount and screw-top, 65 mm high, *c.*1885. All these most probably made in Germany for the English market. *below c. and r.* Island of Jersey souvenir bottle, similar to Goss-china, maker A. B. and C., Birmingham 1905; egg-shaped bottle decorated with swallows, English.

ART NOUVEAU BOTTLES

One is tempted to devote a substantial chapter of this book to a movement which led to the creation of what future historians may well describe as the last International European style, variously known as *art nouveau, Jugendstil, Sezession,* or *le style moderne.* Born out of the English Arts and Crafts Movement based on the revolutionary ideas of William Morris and his circle, it lasted from about 1880 to 1914. Total rejection of the increasing industrialization of the crafts during the 19th century was the movement's motive, and a bridging of the resulting gulf between the crafts and the fine arts its main aim. The thought behind the movement was by no means limited to aesthetic considerations, and much of it derived from a socio-political philosophy demonstrated by the expression of such views as 'the rich must learn to love art more than riches' (Morris). It seems ironic that most of his tangible work was, because of its singularity, so expensive that only the rich could afford it.

Art nouveau is not easy to define: it assimilated numerous styles ranging from the Gothic to the Oriental, and it was catholic in the general sense. Its spirit pervaded painting, sculpture, poetry and drama. The impact of the movement on the making of fine glass changed the entire pattern of production throughout Europe. The industry rid itself of traditional forms and the habit of decorating glass in ways often foreign to the material, largely based on methods of decorating pottery and porcelain. For scent bottles in glass we should first turn to France where, after an almost complete decline, the work of a few ingenious craftsmen led to a veritable renaissance in the creation of art glass.

Towering above all his contemporaries is Emile Gallé of Nancy (1846–1904). The son of a designer of fine faience and furniture—his mother came of a glass-making family—he had the rare fortune of being a man with a suitable background thrown into an optimal environment. After initial training in his father's firm he went to Germany, where he spent several years studying glass technology. The outbreak of the Franco-Prussian war forced him to return to his native land, and he settled at Saint-Clément to make pottery in the regional idiom. Two years later we find him in England as a studious visitor to the South Kensington Museum and, most important, the Royal Botanic Gardens at Kew. Towards the end of 1874 he finally settled in Nancy where he devoted the rest of his life to glass-making. His thoroughness is without comparison in the history of glass-making: not only was he aware of past techniques—some of his earliest work is modelled on 17th-century German glass—and styles, but he also studied chemistry and took great pains to familiarize himself with plant and animal life. No biologist will ever discover discrepancies in his rendering of flowers and insects. That he himself regarded each individual piece as a work of art can be deduced by the fact that he never failed to add his signature to it. Despite this attention to detail and the meticulous finish of his glass his total output is remarkable. Most of his glass is made in the overlay technique but in his case it is inspired by Far Eastern examples rather than Roman or Bohemian. The inner layer is usually semi-transparent and slightly coloured; the cut outer layer is darker in colour (mostly blackish, brown or sepia) and, in most cases, opaque: the figures thus stand out silhouette-like against the light background.

In contrast to the technique employed in overlay glass of earlier periods, the individual layers were not necessarily of the same colour consistency throughout. By the use of enamel paints, gold powder and metal oxides he often achieved surprising colour contrasts. Sometimes he achieved interesting irregularities of colour by reheating part of the surface over the blow-lamp. In no instance does the decorative element clash with the shape of the vessel to which it is applied. The *art nouveau* principle of unity of shape and ornament was hardly ever better realised than in the work of Emile Gallé. The sinuous plant motifs always harmonize with the shape of the vessel and one cannot help but feel that he chose his plant specimen according to the shape of the article he wished to embellish: tall trees or lilies on slender vases, climbers on slender-necked flasks, arching fern fronds and water plants on bowls and shallow flasks (fig. 140) and so on. Earlier pieces are cut on the wheel, and later he made much use of acid etching.

Gallé scent bottles, however, are very rare indeed; the finest example I have seen is illustrated in fig. 141, all the others being either cologne bottles or toilet water sprays. Even rarer are examples in the so-called *Mondscheinglas* (*clair de lune* glass) made around 1880; these bottles are in clear glass with a very delicate enamel decoration and a fine piece is illustrated by G. Gros-Galliner.[25] Emile Gallé's signature is usually of a dark colour and cut in relief. Glasses not made by his own hand are inscribed *cristallerie d'Emile Gallé. Modèle et Décor déposés.* All pieces signed 'E. Gallé' or 'Emile Gallé' are supposedly executed by him but I would not be prepared to vouch for this information. In my opinion there are far too many with this signature for the assertion to be true. In earlier pieces his signature appears in ordinary lettering near the bottom; after 1900 he adopted a more exuberant calligraphic style which frequently forms part of the decorative design.

Gallé's two contemporaries, Eugène Rousseau and Joseph Brocard, both leading figures in the development of *art nouveau* glass, are of no concern within our terms of reference: I have no knowledge of scent bottles made by them. The brothers Daume were strongly influenced by Gallé's work and the scent bottle in pl. XII may be theirs. Among the foreigners who worked with Gallé for some time the two most notable were the Austrian Ludwig Lobmeyr and the American Louis Comfort Tiffany.

An enamelled glass scent bottle made by Lobmeyr (1864–1902) is illustrated by K. Middlemas.[26] A new technique of glass embellishment known as broncit decoration, and consisting of geometrical patterns in matt blackish tones, was

Fig. 140. Two perfume atomizers. *left* Stemmed glass bottle, with foot and upper part acid-etched and heavily part-gilded. Spanish (De Vilbis of Toledo). *right* Conical bottle in opaque glass with purplish overlay decoration, signed E. Gallé. French (Nancy). 152 mm high. Both early 20th century.

developed by Joseph Hoffmann (1870–1955) at Lobmeyr's firm. Broncit decoration has been applied to cologne and toilet water bottles, but these are quite rare.

Louis Comfort Tiffany (1848–1933), a trained jeweller and silversmith turned glass producer, counted among his many types of glass an extremely thin glass with an irridescent metallic surface known in the trade as 'favrile' glass. Tiffany's vessels are excitingly elegant in shape, but one feels, perhaps, that they should have been made in the material they try to imitate in the first place and not in glass. It is hard to find an adjective befitting the Tiffany scent bottle in pl. XIII. It is neither beautiful nor hideous, perhaps provocatively interesting would be the right description. It is just the sort of thing one might expect to have found in the handbag of an American millionairess at the turn of the century. The overall design is Moghul inspired, and the glass is reminiscent of certain Chinese snuff bottles, with a faint influence of Gallé's overlay technique discernible. I doubt whether the great man would have approved of it.

A survey of glass scent bottles cannot be concluded without paying tribute to the man who first manufactured scent bottles of high artistic quality on a large scale for the perfumery industry, namely René Lalique (1860–1945). He studied at the École des Arts Décoratifs and opened a jewellery shop in the Place Vendôme in 1890. Experimenting initially with methods of making paste jewels, he gradually turned his attention to glass-making. Having established himself as an important jewellery designer, Lalique was able to buy a small glass-house near Paris in 1909, and it was there that he started making scent

Fig. 141. *Art nouveau* flacon with silver mount. Decoration of water-lilies in green and purple overlay on opaque marbled orange-grey glass. Engraved signature: Gallé. Silver mounts with applied gilt leaves and flowers, maker's mark A.C. with trumpet. French (Nancy), *c.*1890. 110 mm high. *Kunstgewerbemuseum, Cologne*

Fig. 142. Scent bottle in clear glass; ground stopper extended into the bottle and taking the shape of a thinly veiled female figure. French (Lalique), early 20th century. 150 mm high. *R., Frankfurt-Main*

Fig. 143. Perfume spray in clear glass, decorated in high relief with female nudes in progressive dance movements; mount and upper section in gilt metal. French (Lalique), early 20th century. 93 mm high.

bottles, at first at the request of M. Coty. He was to continue to turn out these items for the next thirty years. Whereas colour was an important element in Gallé's work, in that of Lalique it was almost totally irrelevant, being used only occasionally and then only sparingly. No other glass maker of the period was able to exploit so successfully the elementary characteristics of the material; for him glass existed artistically in its own right and was not to be used as a canvas or vehicle for other materials. The transparency, luminosity and brilliance of glass, so often obscured by surface ornament, were heightened by increasing the refractive surfaces through sculpture cut in high relief. Contrasts of light and shade were created by surface treatment of the cast vessels; matt or even rough sculptural details, most often achieved by sandblasting, were highlighted by polishing the surrounding areas. Although Lalique, like Gallé, derived his decorative themes from nature, he built his motifs into designs of monumental character; some of his creations may be described as architectural (fig. 49). Lalique perfume flacons, appropriately enough in view of the stimulating nature of their contents, pay homage to Venus in their theme of decoration: the female form, nude or thinly veiled, graces many of them. One feels that these delightfully seductive objects could only be French and of that period, reflecting as they do the spirit of the *belle époque* in this great capital of civilized living.

Two of the greatest dancers of the Paris of his day fired Lalique's imagination: Loie Fuller and Isadora Duncan, the former renowned for a dance which she performed lightly veiled and on an ingeniously illuminated stage, the latter for her Greek-inspired style of dancing. Isadora Duncan is often represented, characteristically barefoot, on his scent bottles, toilet water sprays and lamp standards. Particularly attractive are the cylindrical perfume sprays of rectangular panels, each of which bears a representation of a woman in the various attitudes of her dance (fig. 143). The fact that Lalique's patterns were repeated, unlike the unique pieces by Gallé, does not detract from their artistic merit; his work demonstrated that industrially produced glass could still be beautiful.

Lalique's smaller flacons are distinguished by their stoppers, entrancing if not always very practical, which are often in the form of graceful birds spread-

Fig. 144. Scent bottle in slightly matt glass, decorated in high relief with a pair of dancers in diaphanous garments surrounded by flowers. French (Lalique), early 20th century. 93 mm high.

Fig. 145. Scent flask in matt glass, with intaglio decoration of Greek-inspired dancers. French (Lalique), early 20th century. 153 mm high.

ing their wings. A fine example is the well-known bottle consisting of twin dolphins arranged in such a way that their tails form the top of the flacon. There is no doubt that Lalique's creations, and this applies equally to the work of other French artists in the field of design, greatly benefitted the French perfume trade and helped it to maintain its undeniable superiority (figs. 144, 145).

Chapter 4
Bottles in Materials other than Glass

BOTTLES IN METAL AND PRECIOUS STONE

Scent bottles in precious metals were made by goldsmiths and silversmiths all over Europe during the 16th and 17th centuries before being gradually, though never completely, replaced by cheaper materials, mainly glass. Many of them were undoubtedly commissioned pieces. If one discounts 19th-century silver bottles it can be said that metal flasks—unlike bottles in the commoner materials—were never manufactured. This applies equally, of course, to bottles in semi-precious stone. Each individual piece shows great craftsmanship and every known technique has been lavished on these delightful objects, only a few of which can be attributed to a certain master. To describe them in detail would amount to a treatise on metalwork. In this book an attempt has been made to illustrate a fair number of more unusual bottles and smelling boxes not easily accessible to the general public. Fine specimens can also be seen in the jewellery gallery of the Victoria and Albert Museum and the Musée du Louvre in Paris. The number of known bottles for each period reflects the extent to which perfume was used at the time.

The earliest known metal bottles date from the latter part of the 16th century and are either Italian or German in origin. Whether any of them were made in Benvenuto Cellini's workshop is open to speculation. Many gold bottles of this period were enriched by enamelling. A superb gold repoussé bottle of central European origin is seen in fig. 146. I should also mention a fine 16th-century gold and enamel bottle set with rubies and chalcedony panels, attributed to an English craftsmen and to be seen in the London Museum,[27] and a rather pretentious double scent bottle cum watch carved in aventurine and lavishly mounted in gold, which is signed W. Biefield London and exhibited in the Musée Cognac-Jay in Paris. The output of German metalwork during the 17th century and part of the 18th, mainly at the centres of Augsburg and Nuremberg, borders on the miraculous; fine examples of scent bottles are illustrated in figs. 35, 36, 147–150.

Rich deposits of precious and semi-precious stones favoured the development of German stone carving which has continued to the present day since the Middle Ages. One of the most important centres is in the area of Idar-Oberstein in the Taunus mountains. Examples of this highly developed art are seen in the plethora of carved boxes and scent bottles extant, most of them furnished with metal mounts of an equally high standard of craftsmanship (see pls. II and XIV and figs. 151–153). There is also a great tradition in stone carved *objets*

Fig. 146. Repoussé gold bottle with representations after the painters Bartholomäus Sprengel and Hans von Aachen. Prague (court workshop), last quarter of 16th century. 130 mm high. *DROM-Schatzkammer*

Fig. 147. Globular smelling box on domed foot; hinged lid with chased rocailles and flower motifs; handle formed of an acorn and four leaves. Inscription on lower part: Geschenk Friedrichs des Grossen. 1786. German (marked CLP, date mark 1761–1776, Breslau). 115 mm high. *Otto F. Ernst, Wiesbaden*

Fig. 148. Silver-gilt scent bottle overlaid with open-work silver; stopper with amethyst finial. German (Magdeburg), 1st half of 18th century. 140 mm high. *DROM-Schatzkammer*

Fig. 149. Repoussé silver scent bottle with scallop motif. Unidentified maker's mark. German, *c.* 1725. 84 mm high. *J.M., London*

Fig. 150. Chased silver flacon set with semi-precious stones. The heart-shape suggests a bridal gift. Austrian/Bohemian, 2nd half of 18th century. 100 mm high. *Schwarzkopf, Hamburg*

Fig. 151. Smelling bottle in rock crystal with richly ornate silver-gilt mount; hinged lid with pearl finial. French, late 17th century. 50 mm high. *DROM-Schatzkammer*

Fig. 152. Silver-mounted heart-shaped scent bottle in rock crystal, suspended from a silver chatelaine. German, 18th century. 150 mm high (including chain). *DROM-Schatzkammer*

Fig. 153. Rock crystal scent bottle
with stopper in elaborate gilt
mounts, taking the form of a
monstrance. German (Bavarian?),
1st half of 18th century. 120 mm
high. *DROM-Schatzkammer*

Opposite page
Fig 154. Malachite scent bottle with silver-gilt mount and stopper; original leather case. French or Russian, mid-19th century. 90mm high *DROM-Schatzkammer*

Fig. 155. Cylindrical silver-gilt scent bottles, richly decorated and set with pearls and turquoises. Russian. *c.* 1850. 120mm high. *DROM-Schatzkammer*.

Pl. XXV. Porcelain scent bottle of typical rococo form with gilded scrolled edges and finely painted harbour scene. German (Meissen), *c.*1740–45. Approx. 128 mm high. (*Reproduced by kind permission of Hugo Morley-Fletcher*)

Pl. XXVI. 'Provender for the Monastery'. Porcelain bottle in the form of a Franciscan friar carrying a girl concealed in a wheatsheaf. Typical of defamatory representations of monastic life in a province dominated by Protestantism. German (Meissen), *c.*1750. 80 mm high. *DROM-Schatzkammer*

d'art in Russia;[28] the bottle in fig. 154 may have been made in that country.

Fine boxes and scent bottles were made in Denmark from the 17th century onwards, and also in the region south of its border where the craft was centred on the comparatively unknown German city of Tondern. A pair of superb gold and enamel bottles made by Johannes Melchior Dinglinger (1664–1731), similar in shape to the English (?) gold bottle in fig. 156, is in the royal collection at Rosenborg Castle in Copenhagen.[29] For other examples see figs. 37 and 157. Another fine engraved silver scent bottle, made around 1680 and bearing the monograms of Christian V and his Queen, is in the Rosenborg Castle Collection.[30]

It was in 18th-century France that the most exquisite and costly metal scent bottles were made. Ladies of the court of Louis XV did not possess merely one scent bottle but one for every occasion, for each time of day, for each perfume and for each costume (indeed the scent bottle and, in the case of the gentlemen, the snuff box had to be selected carefully so as to harmonize with those items in one's wardrobe with which it was to be worn). The gold and enamel bottle in pl. XV is one example. Many similar flacons, usually of the same flattened pear shape and decorated in all possible techniques with rococo scrollwork, bird and animal representations and the customary *chinoiserie* themes, may be seen in various public and private collections. Most of these bottles are the work of goldsmiths, usually Parisian, notably Jacques Meyboon, Jean Baptiste François Chéret, Martin Langlois, Louis-Joseph Prévot, Charles-Thomas Coutellier. An interesting cast silver bottle, attributed to a Rheims silversmith, is seen in fig. 70.

Following the trend at Versailles quite a profusion of gold and stone-carved bottles were produced in England (pl. XVI and fig. 156). Numerous egg-shaped scent bottles carved in Blue John were made from the late 18th century.

Perhaps the most luxurious piece, a permanent loan to the British Museum, is a gem-studded gold bottle with *ciselé* flowers.[31]

Only brief mention can be made of the many work-cases and *nécessaires* in precious metals, and also in mother-of-pearl, lacquer, jasper and other stone, which were intended to contain, among other items, scent bottles. Some superb specimens are in the Victoria and Albert Museum (Schreiber Collection and the jewellery gallery), the Musée des Arts Décoratifs and the Musée Cognac-Jay in Paris.

Throughout the second part of the 18th century a great number of glass scent bottles, either in coloured glass (ruby red, green or blue) or more rarely in clear glass, were overlaid with gold or silver-gilt cagework, a combination of glass and metal which is most successful. The earliest examples are German and the cagework almost always encloses ruby red glass. Later the technique spread to France, and to England where the finest pieces are attributed to James Cox.

To a lesser extent glass bottles were encaged in metal filigree work, a technique which was practised all over Europe, from Portugal to Scandinavia. It is virtually impossible to attribute the few existing scent bottles of this kind to any one country with certainty. A fine piece is on show in the Victoria and Albert Museum, and another example, perhaps the best in any collection, is seen in fig. 159. (I have not succeeded in identifying the device which forms part of the decoration of this piece.) In this context I should also mention two gilt encaged bottles in pl. IXg and h. In both cases the gilt metalwork is a peculiar mixture of *cloisonné* and filigree in floral and foliate motifs. The provenance of these bottles is a mystery; they are referred to as Venetian or Spanish in some catalogues, and an authority on metalwork recently suggested to me that they could have been made in China for the English market. The patterns are certainly not European, but I believe the glass bottles to be English on account of their quality and shape. Bottles of this type are relatively rare but existing examples are often still accompanied by their (European) leather cases.

Fig. 157. Smelling box in the shape of a handled urn; silver (internal surface gilded); engraved with formal patterns and embellished with 21 diamond-cut glass 'gems'. Danish (Peter Johann Petersen), c.1833. 110 mm high. *DROM-Schatzkammer*

Fig. 158. Dagger-shaped scent bottle in red jasper, harnessed in exuberant chased silver open-work and set with rubies. French, 18th century. 145 mm long. *DROM-Schatzkammer*

Fig. 159. Flattened pear-shaped scent bottle in clear glass, encased with gold filigree; unidentified device. Mediterranean or Turkish, 17th/18th century. 120 mm high. *DROM-Schatzkammer*

ENAMEL BOTTLES

The art of enamelling can be traced back to ancient cultures. We know of enamelled artifacts made by the Egyptians and Assyrians, and a description of the art of *champlevé* enamelling is to be found in the writing of Philostratus (Eikones 1:28) of about A.D. 240. Enamelling materials do not differ essentially from those used in the decoration of pottery: finely ground glass, pigments (metal oxides) and a flux. Four different techniques are identifiable: *champlevé*, *cloisonné*, *basse-taille* and painted enamels. In *champlevé*, enamelling troughs or cells are carved into the surface of the metal, the raised surface between them forming the outlines of the desired pattern. The depressions are filled with the powdered enamel mixture which is then fused in the kiln. The surface is afterwards treated with a corundum file, smoothed with pumice and finally polished with crocus powder and rouge. In *cloisonné* enamel the cells are formed by soldering metal wires on to the plate (fig. 160). These techniques are found in a number of Oriental *brûle-parfums* and in toilet water sprinklers. A third technique, which developed out of *cloisonné*, is termed *plique à jour*; roughly speaking it is a *cloisonné* without a metal background and is used effectively in jewellery design.

Basse-taille enamelling demands great skill, since it is applied to a metal surface into which the intended design is worked in low relief. The enamel

Fig. 160. Gilt metal bottle with floral motifs in *cloisonné* enamel, set with pearls and amethysts; stopper of lapis lazuli. Russian, 19th century. 100 mm high. *DROM-Schatzkammer*

133

colours used are translucent and their shadings vary according to the depth of the design. The technique was developed early in the 14th century and widely applied to vessels of all sorts, ecclesiastical objects especially. During the 19th century, which saw a revival of *basse-taille* enamelling, mainly by Viennese craftsmen, a number of fine scent bottles were decorated in this technique; a fine specimen is illustrated in pl. XVII.

The bulk of enamel ware, certainly of enamel scent bottles, is of the painted variety (pl. XVIII). This method was most probably developed by Venetian craftsmen in the 16th century. It consists of covering a metal base—gold, silver or copper—with a thin film of enamel which becomes the base for the painting. Formidable technical problems had to be overcome in the development of this process. The ideal solution was to cover both surfaces of the metal plate with enamel. The blank metal has only a structural role to play: at first glance an enamelled vessel can easily be mistaken for a piece of mounted porcelain. The technique of painting on enamel does not differ basically from that of porcelain painting, and naturally many a craftsman excelled in both fields.

During the 17th century painted enamelling was practised all over Europe. One of the great centres was Limoges where painted enamels had been produced since the early 16th century, but I doubt that any scent bottles were made there. We have to assume that small objects of this nature were produced in the workshops of gold and silversmiths, or as a clockmaker's sideline. This would certainly seem the case with the extraordinary late 17th-century French item in fig. 161 which combines a scent bottle and a watch case. The fish-shaped bottle in fig. 40 is superbly made; it is either French or Italian. On account of their decorative motifs, a number of scent bottles may be attributed to craftsmen of the Low Countries; one example is the heart-shaped specimen in fig. 162 and

Fig. 161. Enamel scent bottle of a flattened globular shape on a short domed gilt foot, with gilt suspensory rings and screw-top; the front with a hinged lid for holding a watch; the interior of the watchcase painted with ruins in a landscape, the exterior with scenes in the manner of Teniers. French, 2nd half of 17th century. 56 mm high. *Sotheby & Co.*

Fig. 162. Heart-shaped enamel scent bottle painted with a fruit basket and flowers. Dutch (?), mid-17th century. Approx. 50 mm high.

another the double-gourd bottle in fig. 163 with its appealing flower decoration.

With the approach of the 18th century, the rising popularity of perfume was reflected in the increased number of scent bottles made, and during the first half of that century another factor played an important part in the increase in enamel ware: it became a cheaper rival to porcelain, the making of which had been rediscovered at Meissen earlier in the century.

The main centres of enamelling in Germany during the first half of the 18th century were Augsburg and Berlin. Both produced enamelled ware of high quality, as demonstrated by the fine boxes which can be attributed to these places. To what extent scent bottles were made in either town is difficult to ascertain, but there are a few pieces which can safely be attributed on stylistic grounds to the firm of Fromery in Berlin. Enamel boxes signed Fromery (they usually bear the inscription *Fromery à Berlin*) are distinguished from most contemporary work by being decorated with relief ornament which is usually silvered or gilded (pl. XIX). Moreover the mounts of his articles are in gold or silver and are of exceptionally high standard. Two superb specimens admirably displaying Fromery characteristics are in the Houbigant collection in Paris;[32] the gourd-shaped bottle in fig. 164 may also be a product of Fromery's workshop.

Pierre Fromery was one of the many French Huguenots who played a vital part in the cultural enrichment of the Prussia of his day, as indeed they did elsewhere. Born in Sedan, he arrived in Berlin in 1668. As a skilled gunsmith and steel engraver, and possessing a sound business sense, he soon made a name for himself and was appointed gunsmith to the Electoral Court. The expansion of his firm brought a thriving *quincaillerie*, a trading genre hitherto unknown to the Berliners, into the city. He and his heirs were granted the privilege of being sole suppliers of uniform buttons to the Prussian army. Anyone with the slightest knowledge of Prussian history will realize how lucrative it must have been to be in such a position. How quickly his business then expanded is shown by the fact that in 1688 he was permitted to build a large shop in the Mühlendamm occupying the site of the old fish market, and a year later yet another substantial site was acquired near the Electoral Palace. By this time Fromery's business was no longer confined to quality guns and sophisticated ironmongery: he manufactured and traded medals and a variety of other items in gold and silver. It is recorded that whole consignments of blank dressing table sets were imported from Augsburg for gilding and enamelling in his workshops. Throughout his life he must have been an extremely industrious man; it is known that at the age of eighty-eight he supplied the King of Prussia with an engraved seal contained in a magnificent box. After Fromery's death in 1695 the firm was handed on to his son, Alexander, an excellent businessman but an artist of less importance than his father. The firm continued until about 1780.

On the evidence of two plaques in the Hamburg Museum, one bearing the signature 'J. H.' on the front and on the reverse an inscription '*se vend chez Fromery et fils à Berlin*', F.-A. Dreier has conclusively shown that they were decorated by Johann Herold, an enameller and maker of boxes who seems to have been working for Fromery before founding his own firm.[33] This man should not be confused with his countryman Christian Friedrich Herold (born in 1700 in Berlin) who most probably served as an apprentice in Fromery's firm before he took up his employment with the Meissen porcelain factory in 1725. He was to become one of the most important enamellers of his time. There is evidence that he undertook commissions from Alexander Fromery and never lost touch with him; this is indeed not surprising in view of Alexander Fomery's documented trade with Meissen.

Beyond this we do not know much about enamel painters in either Berlin or Augsburg. Research into the question is hampered by the fact that firms in both centres—and this was also the practice of porcelain firms—commissioned

Fig. 163. Enamel scent bottle in the shape of a double gourd, painted with a variety of flowers in the Chinese style; the dividing gold ring is set with rubies. German or Dutch, mid-17th century. 48 mm high. *Sotheby & Co.*

work from outside artists. The decoration executed by the latter is known as *Hausmalerei*. As the connoisseurs of this art will testify, most work of this nature is, even if not always of the same high standard, of much greater spontaneity and it differs markedly from the routine work produced in the factory studios. It also fetches higher prices on today's antique market. Most of the artists employed on *Hausmalerei* are unknown and many a fine piece of enamel work will never be attributable, a fact which by no means diminishes its intrinsic value. All too often a signature only serves the purpose of putting a higher price tag on a piece when it comes on to the market.

Whereas the art of enamelling was widely practised in Europe throughout the 17th century, the history of English painted enamels does not in the main go back much further than the mid-18th century. If one discounts certain minor workshops, the main centres of enamelling were Battersea, Bilston, Wednesbury and Birmingham. This is not the place to delve into the old but somewhat academic arguments as to the attribution of certain specimens of this art. There was a time when all fine English enamels were supposed to have been made at Battersea, but as late as 1924 this belief was undermined by Bernard Rackham when he produced the second edition of the catalogue to the Schreiber Collection. The story of the controversy has been succinctly told by Robert Charleston.[34] The Battersea enamel factory was established in 1752 by Stephen Janssen (later Sir Stephen) at York House, Battersea. After a mere three years it had to close down because of Janssen's bankruptcy. But there is no proof that scent bottles were produced by this short-lived enterprise.

It seems certain that enamelled objects were produced in South Staffordshire before 1750. The most important manufacturer of fashionable enamelled luxuries, known indeed as toys, was John Taylor (1711–75) of Birmingham. His list offered gilt-metal buttons, snuff boxes and numerous other fancy enamelled objects. He was also involved in the production of flint glass in Stourbridge. The measure of his success—and the nature of his character—is revealed by a communication in 1775 from James Watt to Matthew Boulton,

Fig. 164. Gourd-shaped silver enamel scent bottle with silver stopper and suspensory ring. German (Berlin?), early 18th century. 45 mm high. *Städtische Kunstsammlungen, Augsburg*

the great Birmingham industrialist, to the effect that 'John Taylor died the other day worth £20,000 without ever doing one generous action'.

There are at least six major enamel manufacturers around Birmingham and Bilston, such as Dovey Hawksford, who is mentioned as an enameller in 1748, John and Benjamin Bickley, Isaac Becket (father and son), Samuel Yardley and most probably Matthew Boulton himself. It is, however, virtually impossible to attribute enamel scent bottles to any particular firm. Not only the manufacture but the locality is hard to determine. Neither shape nor decoration show any variation which would enable us to attribute items to Birmingham or Bilston. In many instances the artist who executed the main part of the decoration may have worked on a free-lance basis and received commissions from different firms. It is also likely that in elaborate pieces more than one craftsman was responsible for their decoration. Moreover, the copper blanks as well as the mounts were probably produced in one district and enamelled in another.

As one becomes familiar with the entire field of enamel production in 18th-century England one is astonished not only by the high degree of both craftsmanship and ingenuity lavished on these luxurious trifles, and also by the almost complete lack of native originality. Almost everything was made in imitation of earlier or even contemporary Continental ware. One searches in vain for that distinctive Englishness which comes to the fore in English glass of the same period. The reason for the imitation can be seen in the vogue for French elegance and extravagance among the moneyed classes of Georgian England, reflected in the manners, rituals and dress of the period. Also, one has to bear in mind that the manufacturers of these trifles were astute businessmen, eager to cater to a wide market: most English enamels were exported to the Continent. (This thriving trade went into a sudden decline when Napoleon stopped the import of English enamels and the Government of Prussia levied a prohibitive duty on them.)

It is perhaps in English enamel, and this is markedly exemplified by enamelled scent bottles and *bonbonnières*, that one witnesses one of the few instances where the rococo style really took root in this country. The genius of the rococo, alien to the Englishman's temperament and philosophy of life, on the whole suffered the fate of a stranded fish on the chilly shores of these islands.

The *esprit nouveau* of the Dixhuitième transformed any material into fantasies of one kind or another and showed delight in colour, asymmetry, flaming cartouches and startling rocaille ornaments based on shells, water, rock and floral motifs (see pl. XX and figs. 165, 166). Rococo ornament is exuberant without being grotesque, sensuous without being vulgar. It is music translated into colour and shape. No other style radiates so much zest for life, reflects the subtler pleasure of gracious living and epitomises earthly happiness. It was in this period of ultimate taste that the art of perfumery reached its greatest height.

Most pictorial representations on English enamel scent bottles, and this applies to the majority of other objects, are adaptations, or even straight copies, of contemporary paintings or prints. Looking at a large collection of English 18th-century enamel, such as the Schreiber Collection in the Victoria and Albert Museum is like visiting a gallery of French 18th-century pictures in miniature. Subjects by painters such as Watteau, Boucher, Lancret, Vernet and Nattier, predominate and others are borrowed from engravers such as Simon François Ravenet, Jean Daulle, C. Grignion, P. Aveline and François Vivares.

Another pictorial element, certainly applied to enamel wares destined for the home market, consists of portraits. These either were copied from portrait paintings or taken second-hand from engravings or, more often, mezzotints which were then enjoying great popularity. When identifiable personalities are depicted (fig. 167) one may assume that the piece was commissioned, except perhaps where a familiar portrait appears on many and varied objects. The

Fig. 165. Pear-shaped enamel scent bottle, painted with a shepherdess against a background of classical ruins. English (most probably South Staffordshire), c.1760. Approx. 90 mm high. *Victoria and Albert Museum (Schreiber Collection)*, (*Crown Copyright*)

Fig. 166. South Staffordshire enamel scent bottle in the shape of a boy. 3rd quarter of 18th century. Approx. 70 mm high. *Victoria and Albert Museum (Schreiber Collection)*, (*Crown Copyright*) (In the same collection there is a fine Chelsea porcelain scent bottle in imitation of this one but with the stopper taking the form of a bunch of flowers, c.1765.)

137

portrait, in addition, is often of an allegorical nature: on scent bottles we often find graceful representations of Richard Houston's mezzotint series 'The Seasons', based on engravings by Philippe Mercier (1680–1760).

While most of the decorators remain anonymous, a few engravers who worked for the enamelling trade are known to us. First and foremost is the Frenchman Simon François Ravenet (1706–74) who, having settled in England, worked mainly for the publisher Boydell. His work on enamel seems, however, to have been solely with the Battersea factory. Another figure, unknown as an engraver but important as a decorator of Worcester porcelain and English enamel, is Robert Hancock. He had learnt his trade at Battersea and worked also at Bow. Until 1759 he was supervisor of the print department of the Worcester factory as well as a partner in the firm. Some of his enamel prints are signed 'R.H.f.' and a few can be traced back to a book of his engravings in the British Museum. Most of his work is based on that of other artists, for example, the Frenchman Louis P. Boitard.

Advertisements from 1751 and 1752 reveal the name of one Abraham Seeman, a member of a German family well known as enamel painters. He settled in the High Street, Birmingham, advertising himself as an 'enamelling painter'. But we shall never know the identities of those artists mentioned by John Taylor, before a subcommittee of the House of Commons, in 1759: 'There are two or three drawing schools established in Birmingham . . . and thirty or forty Frenchmen and Germans are constantly employed in drawing and designing. . . .' English enamel was thus not only influenced but partly designed by foreign talent.

The artistic possibilities of enamelling are to a large extent dictated by the size of the available painting surface. The really superb pictorial representations are therefore to be found on objects such as the lids of needlework boxes, snuff boxes, plaques, canteens, spill vases and the like. Scent bottles are small and usually of a shape which makes only the lower half available to the painter, whose skills are taxed to the limit. Bearing this in mind one is able to appreciate just how much has been achieved. (See figs. 165, 168, 169.) Watteauesque scenes are the most frequently used. These are usually surrounded by scroll-work, which is often raised and gilded, and the rest of the bottle is so composed

Fig. 167. Enamel scent bottle of a flattened pear shape with gilt metal stopper; portrait of Lady Fenhoulet after a painting by Reynolds. English (South Staffordshire), c. 1760. 127 mm high. *Sotheby & Co.*

Fig. 168. Group of South Staffordshire enamel scent bottles. English. 3rd quarter 18th century. 60 mm, 65 mm and 65 mm high. *Victoria and Albert Museum (Schreiber Collection), (Crown Copyright)*

Fig. 169. Two enamel scent bottles with gilt metal stoppers. *left* South Staffordshire bottle of a flattened pear shape; pale blue ground decorated with whitish trellis-work and flower motifs, and a rococo cartouch enclosed by gilt scrolls. 98 mm high. *right* Bilston 'billing dove' bottle; the white ribbon is tied in a lover's knot and inscribed *Nos amoureux coeurs s'éloignent de peurs.* 85 mm high. *Sotheby & Co.*

as to form an extension of the actual picture, thus achieving an almost theatrical effect. Other bottles are decorated with flowers or birds adapted from contemporary natural history prints or flower paintings. There are simple representations of landscapes, views of ports and the portraits already mentioned below.

The South Staffordshire enamelled pieces were not all individually painted. The technique of transfer-printing was often used. The use of this technique on porcelain was supposedly developed by John Brooks, an Irishman, sometime between 1751 and 1753. The method is basically the same as for ordinary engraving, but the engraved copper plate is inked with a mixture of ceramic colour and oil. A print is produced on paper, which is often gummed, and before the ink is allowed to dry the print is pressed against the surface of the vessel to be decorated. After a while it is put into a muffle kiln in order to fuse the design into the enamelled ground. Robert Charleston mentions a slightly different method described by Lady Shelburne, who visited the workshop of John Taylor of Birmingham:

> . . . a stamping instrument managed only by one woman first impressed the picture on paper, which paper is then laid even upon a piece of white enamel and rubbed hard with a knife, or instrument like it, till it is marked upon the box. Then there is spread over it with a brush some metallic colour reduced to a fine powder which adheres to the moist part and, by putting it afterwards into an oven for a few minutes the whole is completed by fixing the colour . . .[35]

In early work the lines achieved by transfer-printing are somewhat irregular and faint but at all times the design thus achieved had to be retouched with a fine brush. The transfer-picture was, of course, in monochrome, and not many pieces were traded in this state, certainly no scent bottles. After the design had been fixed it was painted over with delicate enamel colours, which were in turn made fast by a second firing in the muffle. In other instances the monochrome transfer-print was washed over with a thin layer of translucent enamel, as can be seen in many snuff boxes or enamel plaques. The transfer-printing of line-engraving was supplemented, if not replaced, by the technique of stipple engraving, a technique which the student of the graphic arts associates automatically with the name of Francesco Bartolozzi (1725–1815). Here the design is achieved by dots rather than continuous lines and thus rendered suitable for engraving in miniature. Developed in Italy and France, it was introduced into England by the ill-fated William Ryland (hanged at Tilbury in 1783 for counterfeiting coins) who is remembered for his many stipple engravings after Angelica Kauffmann. The application of stipple engraving, also known as bat-painting, to English enamel began around 1780 after it had been successfully used on ceramic objects for more than a decade.

Most of the English enamel bottles are of the convenient flattened pear shape, a shape already found in earlier French and German bottles (pl. XXI). Influenced by styles in silverware, some of these pyriform bottles have an elegantly shaped foot which might form a lidded patchbox; in this case the lid will usually have an enamel plate. Sometimes the body of the flacon is press-shaped and the resulting sculpturing adds another dimension to the decoration. Far more adventurous are bottles which take the shape of animals and birds, such as the one in fig. 169—a pair of doves perched against each other and united by a ribbon tied in a love-knot.

The combination of patchbox and scent bottle will be found throughout the 18th century; the earliest known examples may be the pieces illustrated in figs. 34 and 67. The use of patches, however, can be traced back to the first quarter of the 17th century. At first they were nothing but a device to hide facial scars, moles or the occasional pimple, but they soon became a fashionable beauty aid. Female ingenuity had achieved the paradox of turning an impediment into an attraction and the patches or 'court plasters' hid nothing. Paintings of the period show ladies wearing several patches at a time.

In Puritan England a bill was introduced as early as 1650 to prohibit 'the vice of painting and wearing black patches and immodest dress in women'. Common sense must have prevailed, however, for the bill never entered the Statute Book and English court beauties could continue to indulge in this harmless custom. The patchbox itself has its own history which has been outlined by others.[36] It had to be handy at all times and, like the scent bottle, was kept on the dressing table or in the reticule. It is not really surprising that the inventive mind of the metalworker made the two items into one. But there was another fashionable combination in the shape of the scent bottle-*bonbonnière*. Perhaps in imitation of Meissen *bonbonnières*, Chelsea porcelain-makers and South Staffordshire enamellers created a variety of these luxurious containers for small breath-sweetening comfits. They usually took the shape of birds, fish or other animals, a veritable Noah's Ark! They were made either to stand on the table or to be carried in a lady's purse, and in a way they represent the feminine equivalent to the snuff box.

In the combined affair the animal shape had to be abandoned for practical purposes: almost invariably the scent bottle cum *bonbonnière* is somewhat taller than the usual scent bottle and consists of two parts of conical shape. They are joined together at the base and hinged on one side. The upper part, usually smaller, becomes the lid containing the scent bottle and the slightly larger part forms the *bonbonnière*. The metal mounts around the rims are so superbly made that the two halves stay closed without any fastening device (pl. XXII). Although this type of enamel container is conventionally described as a *bonbonnière* it is doubtful whether it was always used as such. In the rare instances where the lower part is smaller than the upper it is conceivable that it was used as a smelling box—the lower part would have been filled with a perfume-soaked sponge.

The application of mounts to enamel containers called for particularly careful attention, since the edges of the enamelled surfaces were in constant danger of being damaged, either through wear and tear or because of the intrusion of moisture into hair cracks. As a result every enamel container has a double rim of metal around the edges. As the illustrations testify, these were not just plain metal rims, but were ornamented by various techniques.

All 18th-century mounts were made by hand and this distinguishes them easily from those applied to the 19th-century reproductions. Only in exceptional cases was gold used for the mounts of English enamel scent bottles; it was substituted by much cheaper alloys. The basic material is not of great importance for the appreciation of the finished product since most mounts on enamel bottles were finely gilded. Throughout the ages, until about the middle of the 19th century, the gold coating was achieved by a process called fire-gilding or *dorure d'or moulu*. Gold, and a few other precious metals, virtually do not react with other elements, but when brought into contact with mercury they form a highly unstable compound termed an amalgam. Generally speaking, amalgam is applied in a thin coat to the metal object to be gilded and the object is then exposed to intense heat: the mercury evaporates and the gold is firmly deposited on the surface of the object. Mercury is a highly toxic substance and therefore the process proved to be a considerable hazard to the metalworker's health. As a result, most gilding is now effected by the so-called electro-deposit method, which was introduced and patented by Messrs. Elkington and Mason of Birmingham in 1840.

The achievement of English metalworkers in the making of mounts is even more remarkable when one considers that there was no historic precedent for it; the art had hitherto been the province of French and German craftsmen and had remained so well into the 18th century. No doubt the ingenious Matthew Boulton (1728–1809) played an important part in their production. Early mounts were relatively plain and simple, but as time went by their ornamentation, achieved by all sorts of mechanical contrivances, became more and more elaborate. This is exemplified by the multitude of shapes for the stopper, which always complements the exuberant decorations lavished on the scent bottle itself. They range from simple perforated flattened stoppers to elaborate foliate rococo scrolls or flowers and representations of creatures such as dolphins or birds of prey (see pls. XX, XXII and figs. 165, 168). The stopper is almost always connected to the mount on the neck of the bottle by a gilt chain.

Whereas the art of enamelling gradually declined in England and Germany, the production of enamelled *objets d'art* of distinction was continued throughout the 19th century in France (mainly Paris), Geneva and Vienna. Since none of these centres developed a distinct style of its own it is often difficult to attribute pieces unless they are marked. Most makers of the period adopted the styles of past centuries for their decoration, as is exemplified by many enamel scent bottles and snuff boxes. The charming bottle in fig. 170 could well have been one of the many toys produced in Vienna for sale to the rich foreign tourists frequenting the spas at Karlsbad, Marienbad, Frankenbad and elsewhere.

Switzerland, and Geneva in particular, has always been and still is the greatest centre for watch and clock making. It is not surprising that Swiss enamellers lavished their skill on the decoration of watches: often one is torn between awe for the engineering and admiration for the decoration that embellishes these small treasures. The marriage of art and engineering is not confined to clocks and watches but is enchantingly represented in all sorts of automata, including musical-boxes, singing birds, musical harps and indeed

Fig. 170. Enamel scent bottle
decorated with flowers and cherubs
between stylized flower borders.
Viennese, 19th century. 77 mm high.
DROM-Schatzkammer

Fig. 171. Scent spray in the form of a flintlock pistol. Swiss, early 19th century. 108 mm long. *Sotheby & Co.* A similar piece is in the Musée Cognac-Jay in Paris.

scent bottles, as exemplified by the elaborate mechanized scent bottle illustrated in pl. XXII.

The automaton depicted in fig. 171 is rather bizarre. Here the scent container takes the shape of a pistol; when the trigger is pulled, flower petals protrude from the golden barrel and squirt perfume at the victim of the amiable attack. The handle is enamelled and, like the mouth of the chased barrel, studded with pearls. This extremely costly precision toy was most probably made by the firm of Jacquet-Droz early in the 19th century, and a number of flacons based on similar designs were made by the same factory. A superb piece is exhibited in the Musée Cognac-Jay in Paris.

PORCELAIN BOTTLES

European Porcelain Bottles In the long history of European perfumery and the *objets d'art* which were created in its wake, the role of porcelain amounts to nothing more than an episode, but a glorious one nevertheless. In comparison with glass, the number of bottles made in this coveted material is relatively small, if one leaves aside the many manufactured china bottles of Victorian and Edwardian times.

True, or hard-paste porcelain, as it is called, had been made in China for many centuries. Pieces imported into Europe during the Middle Ages were highly valued and embellished with costly metal mounts by European goldsmiths, as is exemplified by a porcelain bowl imported into Europe around 1440 which is now in the Hessische Landesmuseum in Kassel. Whether any scent bottles reached Europe in these centuries is not known—a selection of 17th- and 18th-century examples of Chinese porcelain bottles is shown in fig. 172. It is not surprising that, from the 16th century onwards, attempts were made in centres of European pottery manufacture to reproduce the Far Eastern product. The exciting tale of their eventually fruitful efforts, however, does not have any relevance to our theme except for the invention of opaque white glass by the Venetians in the course of their experiments.

Briefly, the first true porcelain was made at Meissen after the ingenious Ehrenfried Walther von Tschirnhaus, an outstanding physicist and universally educated man, rediscovered the Chinese secret of its making. He was assisted by an alchemist, Johann Friedrich Böttger. The background story of this discovery and the establishment of the Meissen factory involves the politics and

Fig. 172. Selection of Chinese scent bottles decorated in blue underglaze; the second from the left (110 mm high) is early 17th century, the others 18th century. *DROM-Schatzkammer*

Pl. XXVII. Porcelain scent bottle representing a flirtatious shepherd and a reluctant shepherdess at the base of a tree. German (Meissen), 19th century. 70 mm high. *DROM-Schatzkammer*

the economic and social conditions of Central Europe of the late 17th century; it has been succinctly sold by Hugo Morley-Fletcher and need not be repeated here.[37] Perhaps one should state that the driving force behind the whole enterprise was the mania of a collector, the Elector of Saxony, Augustus the Strong, with his insatiable passion for Far Eastern porcelain. The amount of money he spent on Chinese and Japanese porcelain and its display would amount to millions in today's currency.

The achievement of the factory, in this new medium, within the first fifty years of its foundation was astounding; the Eastern monopoly was broken, and wares of a quality unrivalled even in France were produced. The factory became the inspiration of all European manufacturers in the centuries that followed.

Among the many porcelain toys, such as *bonbonnières*, snuff boxes, cane handles, *nécessaires*, patchboxes, *carnets de bal*, which were the usual accompaniments of gallant 18th-century life, a great number of flacons, often termed essence bottles, were produced. The inexhaustible Meissen factory archives do not, however, yield much information about them, and the late chief archivist of the factory, Otto Walcha, mentions them only in passing in his important work on Meissen.[38] Thus we have to rely on the evidence of pieces from public and private collections.

Naturally enough, the earliest pieces are strongly influenced by Far Eastern shapes and styles of decoration. In the section on *brûle-parfums* the seated Magot figures ('pagodas'), which were produced in Böttger's red stoneware as well as in white porcelain, have already been described.

Some of the earliest scent bottles (pl. XXIV) are reminiscent of the onion-shaped Chinese porcelain bottles of the K'ang Hsi period, others show a similarity to 17th-century German metal flacons. None of these bottles bears

Pl. XXVIII. Porcelain scent bottle
in the form of a dovecote. English
(Chelsea), 2nd half of 18th century.
95 mm high. *DROM-Schatzkammer*

Fig. 173. Double gourd-shaped porcelain scent bottle in a dark lilac ground colour; on the reverse a delicately painted harbour scene. German (Meissen), *c*.1740. 100 mm high. *Victoria and Albert Museum, (Crown Copyright)*

any signature, but the magnificent miniature paintings of harbour scenes may well have been the work of Johann Gregor Herold. The so-called Kakiemon style (named after a Japanese potter) is represented by the bottle in fig. 174 and the one in pl. XXV, entirely European in conception, reflects, with some restraint, the rococo style at its most elegant. In a way this bottle, with its scrolled edges, owes much of its design to contemporary silver work. Bottles of this shape became very popular; they were imitated by many factories throughout the century (fig. 175) and served as a model for the makers of English enamel bottles.

Undoubtedly the most prolific era in porcelain-making at Meissen began in

Fig. 174. Flacon in white porcelain with red dragon pattern and flower decoration in the Kakiemon style (iron red and gold colours). German (Meissen), 1730–1740. 69 mm high. *Bayerisches Nationalmuseum, Munich*

1731 when Johann Joachim Kändler, who was the greatest porcelain modeller of all times, perhaps only rivalled by Franz Anton Bustelli, was engaged by Augustus the Strong. The output of the following twenty years, known as the 'modeller's period', borders on the miraculous. Among the many figures of lovers, shepherdesses, musicians, gardeners, animals, and the famous series of miners, the *cris de Paris* and the various characters from the Commedia del'Arte, so popular in those times, we find scent bottles playing only a minor role. Perhaps the most striking examples among them, however, is one modelled by Kändler himself which is in the form of Harlequin throwing a bunch of grapes; another Harlequin is shown playing cards and wearing a flower-decorated costume. Perhaps the best known and most widely distributed piece is the satirical flacon shown in pl. XXVI which may also have come from Kändler's own hand. There is a curious double flacon, each stopper of which is in the form of a monkey head, and rare examples of pear-shaped flacons decorated with Watteauesque rococo scenes. The amusing bottle in pl. XXVII is probably, on account of its colours and style, of 19th-century origin, but it may be a reproduction of a predecessor.

The secret of porcelain making did not for long remain a Meissen monopoly. The way it was acquired by other interested parties through devious means, defection and intrigue is a story which makes fascinating reading. The earliest rival factory, which managed to produce hard-paste porcelain in 1719 with the help of two defectors from Meissen, Hunger and Stölzel, was established by Claude du Paquier in Vienna. A number of fine scent bottles with moulded relief decoration and superb *schwarzlot* painting, quite unique in style, issued from that establishment (fig. 176).

One of the reasons for the multifarious cultural activities of 18th-century Germany was her political disunity. Whereas in other European countries cultural development was confined to one centre (London, Paris, St Petersburg), each of the many German courts, however small and politically un-

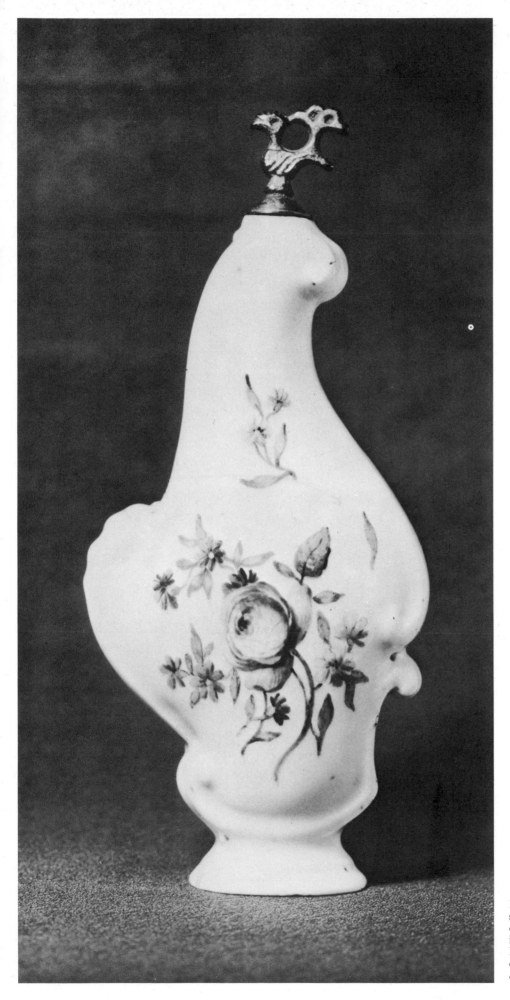

Fig. 175. Porcelain scent bottle with
scrolled edges and 'deutsche Blumen'
decoration; bronze stopper. Clearly
in imitation of a Meissen bottle.
Russian (St Petersburg), 18th
century. 130 mm high. *DROM-
Schatzkammer*

Fig. 176. Two lidded porcelain scent bottles, richly gilded and with cherubs painted in *schwarzlot*. Viennese (Du Paquier), 1718–1744. Approx. 150 mm high. *Österreichisches Museum für angewandte Kunst, Vienna*

Fig. 177. *left* Scent bottle in rococo style. German (Königliche Porzellan Manufactur, Berlin), *c.*1855. *centre* Classical-inspired porcelain flacon with porcelain stopper. German (Thuringian), *c.*1800. *right* Vase-shaped porcelain bottle with hand-painted flower decoration and gilding. German, 1st half of 19th century. *Wella Museum, Darmstadt*

Fig. 178. Porcelain scent bottle in the form of a huntsman, his head forming the stopper, wearing a green cap, green breeches under a puce-lined coat, with his left hand holding a skin bag; gilt metal mount. German (Ludwigsburg), 2nd half of 18th century. Approx. 90 mm high. *Sotheby & Co.*

Fig. 179. Egg-shaped porcelain scent bottle with a view of the Royal Palace at Potsdam (Neues Palais); initials of Wilhelm II on reverse. Porcelain stopper in the form of the Imperial crown. German (Berlin), late 19th century. 95 mm high. *DROM-Schatzkammer*

Fig. 180. Heart-shaped porcelain perfume flask, stopper missing. Italian (De Nove), *c*.1810. Approx. 60 mm high. *Victoria and Albert Museum, (Crown Copyright)*

important, set its own cultural tone. (The lasting effect of this is still recognizable today in, for example, the many excellent orchestras and opera houses in modern Germany). Small wonder that numerous porcelain factories sprang up all over German-speaking Europe. Most of them included scent bottles in their output. After Meissen went into decline, mainly as a result of the defeat of Saxony at the hand of the Prussian monster in 1756, the smaller centres of porcelain making gained in importance. Nymphenburg, which could boast the genius of Bustelli, is not known to have produced any perfume flacons, but the fine perfume burner in fig. 47, though of a later period, is from this factory. Delightful rococo flacons were made at the Thuringian factory of Kloster Veilsdorf, many of them based on characters from the Italian comedy, others in the form of the Three Graces and one showing a boy and a goat beside a tree trunk (a pattern also used at Meissen and Derby). Another flacon is in the form of a squirrel climbing a tree-trunk. A late piece from this factory's vast production is seen in fig. 177. In the Ludwigsburg factory the modeller J. W. C. Beyer was responsible for many fine bottles, and pieces similar to the one in fig. 178 came from the factories of Fürstenberg and Höchst. Many of the so-called fruit flasks, erroneously described as Chelsea, are attributable to Fürstenberg. The short-lived Fulda factory, sponsored by the Prince-Bishop Heinrich von Bibra, was renowned for fine porcelain figures in the rococo style, but none of its scent bottles seems to have found its way into a public collection.

It is not surprising that Frederick II of Prussia (often referred to as 'The Great') established his own porcelain manufacture. Its history is not without interest, but it never succeeded in attaining anything like the position of Meissen at its height. The only 18th-century piece I have seen is in the museum at Sèvres: it is a bottle of a flattened pear shape, attributed to the Berlin factory. During the 19th century a number of scent bottles, some of them depicting palaces and emblems of the Royal Court (fig. 179), were made there.

Outside Germany porcelain scent bottles were made, but on a much smaller

Fig. 181. Pear-shaped porcelain
flacon decorated with pastoral scene
in grisaille colours heightened with
pink. Silver-gilt mounts and hinged
porcelain top. French, 19th century.
110 mm high.

Fig. 182. Globular porcelain scent
bottle with floral decoration, gilt
metal mount and hinged lid. French
(Sèvres), early 19th century. 48 mm
high. *DROM-Schatzkammer*

scale, at Capo-di-Monte,[39] de Nove (fig. 180) and in the French factories at Chantilly and Mennecy. Among the 18th-century bottles produced at Mennecy one finds a number made in the shape of a lady's leg, as exemplified by a superb piece in the Musée des Arts Décoratifs in Paris. During the 19th century France produced large numbers of perfume and cologne bottles in porcelain (figs. 181, 182).

In a book which deals with European scent bottles in general only a small selection of the large number of 18th-century porcelain bottles can be presented; the subject is so vast and the problems of attribution so involved that it should be dealt with in a separate book. I also believe that porcelain scent bottles, especially figurine bottles of the rococo period, were never really a practical proposition. Together with other bibelots mentioned above they were advertised as 'toys' and I am quite certain that they were bought principally for their visual appeal and treasured as collector's pieces in their day. Some may never have contained perfume. This seems to be the only explanation for the surprisingly large number of pieces surviving intact.

English Porcelain Bottles Almost half a century after von Tschirnhaus's successful recreation of porcelain, a porcelain factory was established in England (c. 1745), but it was to take more than another twenty years before true, that is hard-paste, porcelain was in production. Whereas Continental manufacturers relied almost exclusively on royal or princely patronage, the English enterprises were run by businessmen and on strictly commercial lines. This fact becomes relevant when one seeks an explanation as to why scent bottles were produced in an astounding quantity and variety, and why they display stylistic traits so completely alien to the English temperament. One can only assume that to a large extent they were made, like contemporary English enamel ware, for the thriving export market. One must bear in mind, on the other hand, that the driving forces behind the earliest English factories were

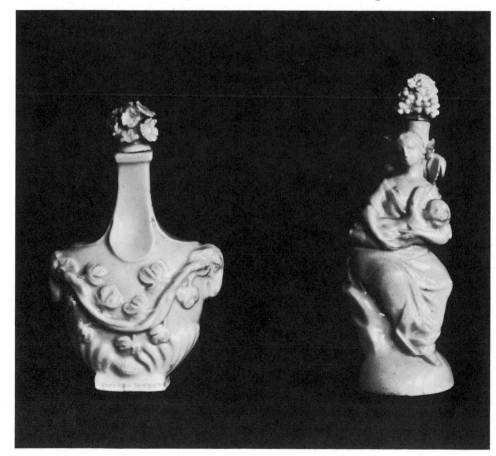

Fig. 183. Two porcelain scent bottles with porcelain stoppers; one with flower decoration, the other in the form of a mother holding her baby. English (Girl in a Swing), 1749–1754. Approx. 70 mm and 80 mm high. *Victoria and Albert Museum (Schreiber Collection), (Crown Copyright)*

Huguenot craftsmen and other *émigré* workers. It is remarkable that, with the possible exception of Wedgwood, the English porcelain industry never actually produced men of genius, such as Kändler and Bustelli, or painters of Herold's standing, yet when it comes to what is known as Chelsea porcelain we have wares which can stand comparison with most of the Continental output. The combination of *émigré* modellers—one should also bear in mind the presence in England of sculptors such as François Roubillac, Michel Rysbrack and Peter Scheemakers—and the technical knowledge of native potters resulted in the creation of porcelain imbued with all the beauty, charm and naive sensuousness of European rococo at its best (pl. XXVIII and figs. 183, 184).

It was at Chelsea that the fame of English porcelain-making was established and one is inclined to agree with H. Tate when he states that none of the porcelain factories which sprang up subsequently 'approached the same degree of excellence found in the best of Chelsea'.[40] Chelsea porcelain must be divided into two groups, since all items known under the name 'Chelsea toys' were not produced at the same factory; in fact quite a number were made at Derby after 1770.

The first Chelsea factory was founded by a Belgian silversmith, Charles Gouyn, and later (after 1749) managed jointly by Gouyn and a silversmith from Liège, Nicolas Sprimont. Internal difficulties led to a split and in 1749 a short-lived rival factory, apparently run by Gouyn, was established in another part of Chelsea. It was this enterprise which produced the most outstanding and elegant Chelsea scent bottles, and it was on account of one of its most famous pieces, the white porcelain figure of a girl in a swing (a subject frequently found in rococo painting) that the firm became known under the rather clumsy name of Girl in a Swing factory. Sprimont's firm continued until it was merged in 1769 with William Duesbury's Derby factory. Scent bottles from Sprimont's original factory are usually put into two fairly distinct categories, namely those of the 'red anchor' period (1752–56) and the 'gold anchor' period (1758–70). A few bottles from either factory show a clear Meissen influence—some, like the Harlequin and Rose bottle, seem to be a most ingenious adaptation of Kändler's famous figure—but the majority, although following the Continental fashion, are independent creations.

Other 18th-century English porcelain factories made scent bottles in relatively small numbers. A Harlequin figure, made at the Bow factory in London, has been recorded[41] and at the Victoria and Albert Museum there is a long-necked onion-shaped flask in blue underglaze decoration of Longton Hall origin which may well have been a scent bottle. A number of late 18th-century bottles with diaper patterns and flower decorations against a pale blue background (signature S H) were made at Derby.

The bottles made at the Bristol factory owned by Benjamin Lund are completely different in shape and style. H. Tate illustrates a most interesting specimen from the British Museum collection, made around 1750, which he believes to be inspired by 'contemporary "Bristol" glass scent bottles with their wheel-cut faceted surfaces'.[42] The difficulty is that Bristol glass bottles were made at least twenty-five years later but, surprisingly the British Museum bottle is almost identical in shape and cutting pattern to the earlier glass bottles previously discussed (fig. 34).

During the 19th century most porcelain factories, Worcester, Derby, Coalport and even Spode, produced scent bottles in numbers which defy classification; some examples are seen in figs. 122, 123, 125.

The man whose scent bottles, in their sober neo-classical elegance, stand out from the products of all other factories of his time, is Josiah Wedgwood. All his bottles were in the so-called blue and white jasper ware, and the style of Greek and Roman classical sculpture (pls. XXIX, XXX). The factory was near Burslem and was given the name of Etruria by Wedgwood and his partner,

opposite page
Fig. 184. Girl in a Swing scent bottles. *above l. to r.* Venus and Cupid with a clock (66 mm high); seated girl holding a basket of grapes (78 mm high); Commedia del' Arte bottle, Harlequin and Columbine (91 mm high). *centre l. to r.* Bottle in the form of a goldfinch (66 mm high); 'billing doves' double bottle (72 mm high); double bottle in the shape of a hen and chicks (69 mm high); *below l. to r.* Pug bottle (63 mm high); bottle in the form of a girl playing the hurdy-gurdy (78 mm high); bottle in the shape of a bouquet of flowers (75 mm high). *Sotheby & Co.*

Thomas Bentley. Opinions on Wedgwood jasper ware are divided: it has its keen admirers and its detractors. The aversion felt by some may be explained by the fact that one sees too much of it, because the factory continued to pour out jasper ware, and does so still today. Unfortunately, after Wedgwood's death the quality of the product declined markedly.

In 18th-century jasper ware, there are two kinds to be distinguished: in the earliest pieces the clay was solidly coloured, but this technique was soon superseded by the so-called jasper dip. In this method the coloured background to the sculpture was achieved either by dipping the jasper body in colour or by brushing colour on to it. Fine 18th-century bottles are very rare and are usually only to be found in museum collections. Jasper ware was so successful and so much acclaimed on the Continent that even during Wedgwood's lifetime copies were produced by various potters in England and later in Germany. Contemporary imitations, mainly made by Turner (fig. 185) and Neale, are often indistinguishable from the genuine article. The easiest way of identifying late 19th- and 20th-century reproductions (German and American) is to ascertain whether the object including sculpture is moulded in one piece; in fine Wedgwood ware the high relief decoration is applied by hand to the body.

Fig. 185. *left* Scent bottle in blue jasper ware, decorated with a profile portrait of the Prince of Wales, later George IV. Probably modelled by John Loche. English (Wedgwood, Etruria), *c.*1790. Approx. 55 mm high. *centre* Bottle in jasper dip ware; on one side the figure of a girl holding a child, on the other a design by Lady Templetown. English (South Staffordshire, probably by Turner), late 18th century. Approx. 85 mm high. *right* Bottle similar to the one on the left, decorated in neo-classical style. *Victoria and Albert Museum, (Crown Copyright)*

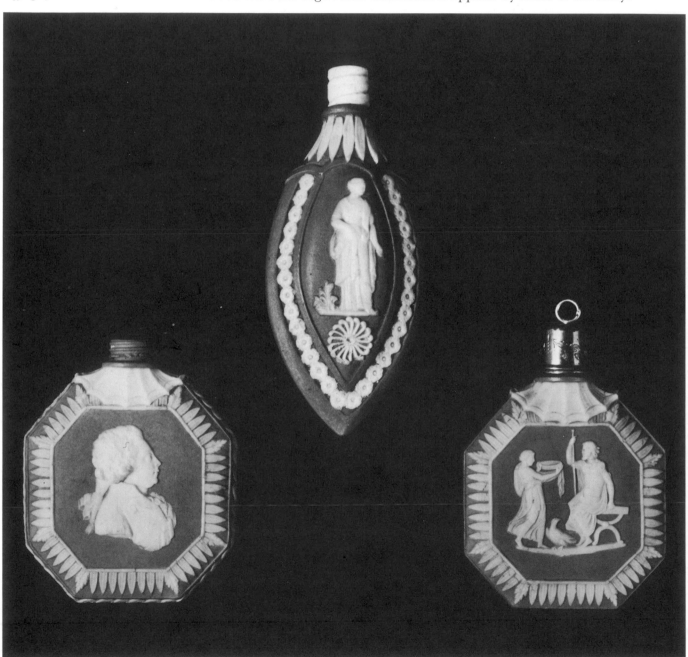

The basic colours of 18th-century jasper ware are black, blue or sea-green; jasper ware with a white background colour and blue sculptural decoration are much rarer, and pieces with a yellow or amber background, even more so.

OTHER MATERIALS

Amber and Ivory Bottles Since larger pieces of amber often exhibit flaws in the form of fissures and cracks, and since the material is in any case very fragile, amber has seldom been used to make scent bottles. Those which have been made successfully originate from the town once known as Danzig, on the Baltic coast. An exquisite piece is shown in fig. 186; it is in the shape of a hunting horn decorated with hunting and martial scenes. Both ends have gilt-metal mounts and the stopper is attached to the base by a chain. A simpler, but nevertheless charming bottle is seen in fig. 187. The one in fig. 188 is rather amusing; it quite obviously represents a woman squatting to relieve herself. Representations of such natural functions have figured in the art of the Low Countries throughout the centuries, witness Bosch and Breugel.

Ivory scent bottles are even rarer than those in amber, the material also being liable to develop cracks. A few fine examples of 17th-century carved flacons are, however, extant. Invariably they represent the human form, the head acting as a stopper—a rather undignified affair. An extremely fine specimen, a double flacon in the form of a courting couple, is seen in fig. 189. Both the style of the carving and the somewhat rustic humour expressed by this piece suggest a Dutch or German origin.

The flacons illustrated in figs. 190–195 are of great interest. They are German, and of the 17th century, but in the absence of signatures they cannot be attributed to a particular region or workshop. Eugen von Philopowich, an authority on ivory carving, does not mention any flacons in his comprehensive work on the subject.[43] But during the 17th century there were in Germany, the Low Countries and Switzerland a number of centres producing sundials, gunpowder flasks and priming flasks in ivory. As for the objects illustrated, there is no doubt that these were used as perfume or smelling bottles, on

Fig. 186. Carved amber scent bottle in the shape usually associated with a priming-flask. Decorated in high relief with the trophies of war and (on reverse) a hunting scene; gilt metal mounts at either end and metal stopper attached to the flask by a chain. German, 17th century. Approx. 95 mm high. *Sotheby & Co.*

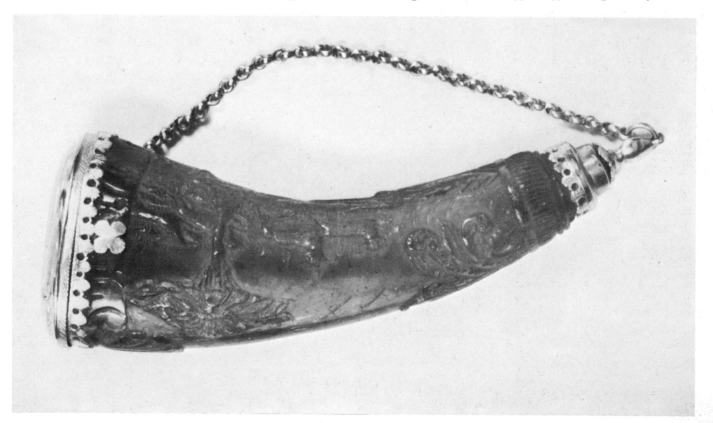

Fig. 187. Amber scent bottle with two compartments and tightly fitting amber stoppers; circular foot of differently coloured amber. This piece was once owned by Sir Hans Sloane. German (?), *c.*1730. Approx 60 mm high. *British Museum (Natural History)*

Fig. 188. Carved amber scent bottle taking the form of a woman relieving herself; the head acts as a stopper. North German or Dutch, 1st half of 18th century. Approx. 60 mm high. *Wella Museum, Darmstadt*

opposite page
Fig. 189. Double scent bottle in ivory, in the form of a seated peasant couple. Flemish, 17th century. 56 mm high. *J.M., London*

158

Fig. 190. Flacon of a flattened oval shape carved in staghorn, showing a gentleman in high relief surrounded by stylized foliage motifs; bronze mounts. German, 17th century. 33 mm high. *Kunstgewerbemuseum, Berlin-Charlottenburg*

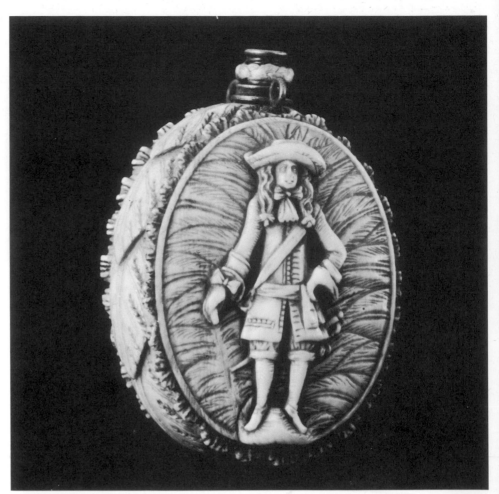

Fig. 191. Reverse of fig. 190, showing a lady. The flacon was most probably a wedding gift.

Pl. XXIX. Scent bottle in blue jasper ware decorated with zephyrs; silver screw-top. English (Wedgwood), 1786. 89 mm high. *DROM-Schatzkammer*

160

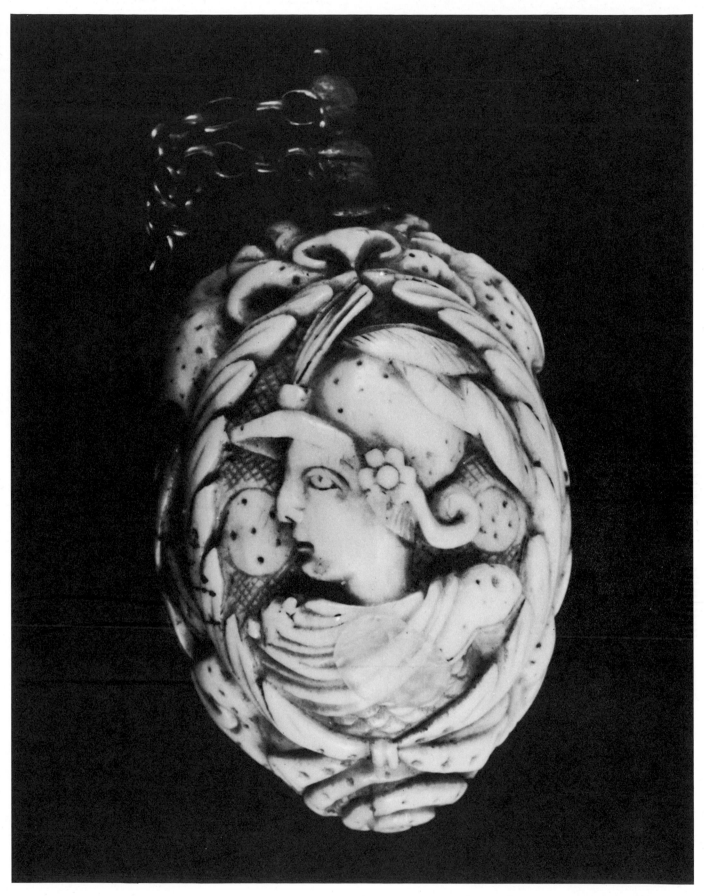

Pl. **XXX**. Scent bottle in blue jasper
ware decorated with *putti*; gold
screw-top and ring. English (Wedgwood), early 19th century. 70 mm
high. *DROM-Schatzkammer*

Fig. 192. Flacon carved in ivory;
formal convolute foliage ornament
with portrait in high relief;
bronze mount and screw-top.
German, 17th century. 68 mm high.
*Kunstgewerbemuseum, Berlin-
Charlottenburg*

Fig. 194. Flacon carved in ivory, depicting two *putti* fighting. German, 17th century. 70 mm high. *Kunstgewerbemuseum, Berlin-Charlottenburg*

Fig. 195. Conical flacon carved in ivory, depicting mythological beasts and figures; turned ivory foot. German (?), 17th century. 86 mm high. *Kunstgewerbemuseum, Berlin-Charlottenburg*

account of their small size and, too, the fact that they were made to stand upright. The flacon illustrated in figs. 190 and 191 is carved in staghorn, a material similar in appearance to ivory which was widely used in Germany for the carved handles of knives and forks, and for small flasks and similar objects.

The art of ivory carving flourished in Dieppe during the 17th and early 18th centuries, but I do not know whether any scent bottles were made there. The 17th-century ivory container in fig. 196 is intriguing; it could be either Venetian or German. For an example of a turned specimen in ivory, see fig. 127.

A material similar to ivory is obtained from the seeds of various palm species belonging to the genus Phytelephas. These seeds are traded as vegetable ivory, coroso or tagua, and have been carved into scent bottles, buttons, toys, small figures, relief portraits, etc. (fig. 127). The plants inhabit damp tropical regions in Ecuador and Colombia. The endosperm of the seed, like ivory, is hard, heavy and easy to cut and polish. Objects in this material soften when immersed in water but regain their hardness on drying; this property makes it readily distinguishable from real ivory. An individual seed is about as large as a hen's egg.

Fig. 196. *left* Turned ivory scent box (base unscrews) in the shape of a beehive, holding a glass phial. Venetian or German, late 17th century. 45 mm high. *centre* Scent bottle made of an exotic seed; silver-mounted neck, base and stopper. European, *c.*1700. 80 mm high. *right* Turned scent bottle in wood (box?) or vegetable ivory, with ivory stopper and handle. European, 1st half of 19th century. 70 mm high. *DROM-Schatzkammer*

Pottery and Alabaster Bottles Both pottery and alabaster are only of marginal interest in connection with scent bottles. In the former, fine cracks in the glazing soon render any perfume worthless, and the weight of the bottles, besides, makes them impractical as portable items for a lady's purse. At best they could be used as smelling bottles, and indeed a number have survived which clearly had this function. Most of them date from the first half of the 18th century and are in either salt-glazed stoneware or, less commonly, agate or marbled ware. Two interesting smelling bottles in glazed iron-brown pottery, dating from around 1740, are preserved in the Stoke-on-Trent Museum.

Scent bottles carved in alabaster are extremely rare. On account of its softness, this substance is not suitable for articles which have to be carried around and handled frequently. Those thin-walled vessels which do, in fact, exist are attractive chiefly on account of their translucency. An exceptionally fine flask is depicted in fig. 197.

Fig. 197. Alabaster scent container with tulip decoration; pewter screw-top. Dutch, 17th century. 100 mm high. *DROM-Schatzkammer*

165

Tortoise-shell Etuis Tortoise-shell has never been used for scent bottles, but there are many 18th- and early 19th-century scent bottle étuis in this material. Strictly speaking they belong to the box category, but in many cases scent bottles and their étuis are perfectly integrated (figs. 198, 199). Tortoise-shell is derived from the thick and horny shell scales of the hawksbill turtle (Chelone imbricata) which inhabits tropical coastal waters of the Western hemisphere. The scales of this large animal—a mature specimen can yield from eight to fifteen pounds—are soft and flexible, and the surface can be polished. Their colour ranges from a bright clear yellow and amber to all tones of brown and near black. They can have tinges of green or blue and may be speckled or spotted. It is not surprising that this beautiful and versatile material has been widely used in the applied arts throughout the centuries. In Europe the best markets for tortoise-shell were Spain, Italy (Naples) and Holland.

Sometimes tortoise-shell is substituted by horn, which has similar properties but which lacks the fine colouring; the application of a paste made of two parts lime to one part litharge and some soda lye will make the imitation more satisfactory. Artificial tortoise-shell is manufactured by melting certain metallic salts with gelatine, but the modern chemical industry has not yet developed an ideal substitute.

opposite page

Fig. 198. *below l.* Wooden hexagonal box with hinged lid and engraved mother-of-pearl panels, containing small cut-glass bottle. English, late 18th century. *below r.* Etui in tortoise-shell set with silver *piqué*-work, containing small cut-glass bottle. English, late 18th or early 19th century. (*also shown: left* Carved wood scent bottle with ivory neck and stopper. German (?), 19th century. *centre* Silver scent bottle with hinged cap and checkboard pattern, glass-lined. French, *c.* 1840–1850. *right* Scent bottle with glass phial inserted into open-cut woodwork, with silver neck and cap. 19th century.) *J.M., London*

Fig. 199. Selection of étuis for holding scent bottles: *above l. and r.* ivory, *centre r.* straw-work; the others, tortoise-shell. English, late 18th/early 19th century.

When heated, both horn and tortoise-shell become malleable and any shape formed, or any pictorial representation pressed into its surface, will be retained after cooling. Box lids with moulded portraits or coats of arms are often found. One of the finest masters of the art was the Huguenot artist John Obrisset who worked in London in the early 18th century. Most étuis for holding perfume flacons are, however, decorated in *piqué*. Horn, and tortoise-shell even more so, are ideal vehicles for this delicate ornamentation in gold or silver. Since the surface of both materials can be softened by heat, the thinly rolled metal need only be pressed into it, and after the cooling and subsequent shrinking of the material the metal will be held in place without the aid of glue or cement. The *piqué* technique, invented by Italian craftsmen, found its first great exponent in Charles Andre Boulle (1642–1732), but most of the *piqué* work found in scent bottle étuis dates from the 18th and early 19th century, when it was produced in quantity all over Europe. In England it gained popularity when Huguenot craftsmen introduced the technique. The following types can be distinguished: *clouté d'or* or nailhead *piqué*, in which the decoration is achieved with large points inset into the surface, and the more refined *piqué point* developed in the early 18th century, in which patterns are created by inserting gold or silver points of different size into the tortoise shell which is then polished. (Perfume étuis of this kind are extremely rare.) The most commonly found technique is *piqué posé*, by which shapes are cut from thin sheets of gold or silver and then let into the surface. An attractive variation of this technique is the hairline *piqué* or hairline *piqué d'or*; as far as I know it was only practised in England and specimens are rare. *Piqué* work came to an end towards the middle of the 19th century, but after 1870 a number of boxes were produced by mechanical means.

Fig. 200. Engraving from the lid of a lady's travelling toilet box. French, end 18th century.
Parfumerie Fragonard, Grasse

Notes

1. Septimus Piesse, *The Art of Perfumery* (1879) 140.
2. Cf. Y. R. Naves et G. Mazuer, *Les parfums naturels* (1939).
3. *The Connoisseur*, April 1934.
4. Cf. Eric Delieb, *Silver Boxes* (1968) 49–50.
5. Cf. W. Turner, 'Silver and plated ware: pomanders', *The Connoisseur*, March 1912.
6. *The Connoisseur*, November 1963.
7. Cf. Delieb, op. cit., 48–9.
8. Cf. L. Hansmann und L. Kriss-Rettenbeck, *Amulett und Talisman* (1966) 64–71.
9. Cf. L. Hansmann und L. Kriss-Rettenbeck, op. cit., 192–207.
10. A. von Saldern, *German Enamelled Glass* (1965) 156, 158.
11. *Spanish Glass* (1963).
12. K. Foster, op. cit., pl. 23.
13. 'Lead in glass,' *Archaeometry*, No. 3, 1960, 1–4.
14. Cf. R. J. Charleston, 'Michael Edkins and the problem of English enamelled glass', *Transactions of the Society of Glass Technology*, 1954.
15. Cf. R. J. Charleston, 'James Giles as a decorator of glass', *The Connoisseur*, June and July 1966.
16. Cf. Ph. Warren, *Irish Glass*.
17. Cf. Ada Polak, 'Sulphides and Medals', *Journal of Glass Studies*, No. 8, 1966.
18. Cf. G. Patzaurek, op. cit.
19. *Nineteenth-Century Cameo Glass* (1956).
20. Op. cit.
21. *Investing in Silver* (1970) 119, 112.
22. Op. cit.
23. *More Small Decorative Antiques* (1962).
24. Op. cit.
25. *Glass* (1970) plate facing p. 145.
26. *Continental Coloured Glass* (1971) 118.
27. Cf. K. Foster, op. cit., pl. 7.
28. Ibid, pl. 83.
29. Ibid, pl. 82.
30. Ibid, pl. 84.
31. Cf. H. Tate, 'An anonymous loan to the British Museum of Renaissance Jewellery', *The Connoisseur*, November 1963.

32. Cf. K. Foster, op. cit., pls. 3 and 33.
33. '*Zwei Berliner Emaillplatten aus der Zeit Friedrichs des Grossen*', *H. d. Hamburger Unterl.*, 1958, Bd. 3.
34. 'Battersea, Bilston—or Birmingham?', *Victoria and Albert Museum Bulletin*, 1967, No. 3, 1–44.
35. Op. cit.
36. *Silver Boxes*, 18–19; *Investing in Silver*, 104–5.
37. *Meissen* (1970).
38. *Meissener Porzellan* (1973).
39. K. Foster, op. cit., pl. 80.
40. *Porcelain* (1966).
41. K. Foster, op. cit., p. 76.
42. *Porcelain*, pl. 29.
43. *Elfenbein* (1961).

Bibliography

Allendry, R. *Le symbolisme des nombres*, Paris, 1921

Amic, Yolande. *L'Opaline française au 19e-siècle*, Paris, 1953

Barbe, Simon. *Le parfumeur françois*, 4th ed., Paris, 1968

Barrelet, J. *La verrerie en France*, Paris, 1953

Bayle, V. *L'amateur de parfums*, Raoul Solar, Grasse, 1953

Beard, G. *Nineteenth-century cameo glass*, Newport, 1956

Bedford, J. *Bristol and other coloured glass*, Cassell, London, 1964

Bellucci, G. *Il feticisuo primitivo in Italia*, Perugia, 1919

Boehn, M. von. *Das Beiwerk der Mode*, München, 1928

Buckley, F. *A history of old English glass*, London, 1925

Delieb, E. *Silver boxes*, Herbert Jenkins, London, 1968

—— *Investing in silver*, Barrie & Rockliff, London, 1970

Dölger, F. G. *Der heilige Fisch in den antiken Religionen*, Münster, 1922

Elville, E. M. *The collector's dictionary of glass*, Country Life, London, 1961

Ferguson, J. *Bibliotheca chemica*, London, 1954

Foster, K. *Scent bottles*, *The Connoisseur* monograph, London, 1966

Frothingham, A. W. *Spanish glass*, Faber & Faber, London, 1963

Gross-Galliner, G. *Glass*, Frederick Muller, London, 1970

Hansmann, L. und Kriss-Rettenbeck, L. *Amulett und Talisman*, München, 1966

Havard, H. *Dictionnaire de l'ameublement*, 2nd ed., Paris, n.d.

Haynes, B. E. *Glass through the ages*, Pelican, London, 1964

Horn, E. *Parfüm*, München, 1967

Hughes, Th. *More small decorative antiques*, Lutterworth, London, 1962

Jackson, Sir Charles. *An illustrated history of English plate*, 2 vols, Country Life, London, 1911

Jellinek, P. *Die Psychologischen Grundlagen der Parfümerie*, Heidelberg, 1965

Jokelson, P. *Sulphides*, Nelson, London, 1968

Kämpfer, F. (translated and revised by E. Launert) *Glass, a world history*, Studio Vista, London, 1966

Ladendorff, H. *Der Duft und die Kunstgeschichte*, Festschrift Erich Meyer, Hamburg, 1957

Middlemas, K. *Continental coloured glass*, Barrie & Jenkins, London, 1971

Morley-Fletcher, H. *Meissen*, Barrie & Jenkins, London, 1970

Naves, Y. R. et Mazuer, G. *Les parfums naturels*, Paris, 1939

Patzaurek, G. *Gläser der Empire- und Biedermeierzeit*, Klinkhardt & Biermann, Leipzig, 1923

Pellatt, A. *Curiosities of glassmaking*, London, 1849

Philipowich, E. von. *Elfenbein*, Braunschweig, 1961

Piesse, S. G. W. *The art of perfumery*, 4th ed., London, 1879

—— *Chimie des parfums*, Paris, 1917

Saldern, A. von. *German enamelled glass*, Corning Museum, New York, 1965

Savage, G. *Dictionary of antiques*, Barrie & Jenkins, London, 1970

Schlosser, J. von. *Die Kunst- und Wunderkammern der Spätrenaissance*, Leipzig, 1908

Sinclair, R. *Essential oils*, Unilever, London, 1963

Tate, H. *Porcelain*, Hamlyn, London, 1966

Thompson, C. J. S. *The mystery and lure of perfume*, London, 1927

Thorpe, W. A. *History of English and Irish glass*, London, 1929

Walcha, O. *Meissner Porzellan*, Dresden, 1973

Warren, Ph. *Irish glass*, Faber and Faber, London, 1970

Wenzel, H. *Bisamapfel*, Reallexikon zur Deutschen Kunstgeschichte, Vol. 2, 1948

Werner, I. *Das alemannische Fürstengrab von Wittislingen*, München, 1950

Willdey, George. *General atlas*, London, 1715. (A complete copy is held by the Royal Geographical Society.)

Winter, F. *Der moderne Parfumeur*, Vienna, 1949

Articles

Brückner, W. 'Hand und Heil im "Schatzbehalter" und in volkstümlicher Graphik', *Ant. Germ. Nationalmuseum*, 1965

Charabot, E. et Gatin, C.-L. *Le parfum chez la plante*, Paris, 1908

Charleston, R. J. 'Lead in glass', *Archaeometry*, No. 3, 1–4, 1960

—— 'Souvenirs of the Grand Tour', *Journal of Glass Studies*, No. 1, 1959

—— 'Michael Edkins and the problem of English enamelled glass', *Transact. of the Society of Glass Technology*, 1954

—— 'James Giles as a decorator of glass', *The Connoisseur*, June and July 1966

—— 'Battersea, Bilston—or Birmingham?', *Victoria and Albert Museum Bulletin*, No. 3, 1–44, 1967

Dreier, F.-A. 'Zwei Berliner Emaillplatten aus der Zeit Friedrichs des Grossen', *H. d. Hamburger Unterl.*, Bd. 3, 1958

Gros, G. 'The case for Lalique', *Collector's Guide*, November 1968

Hildburgh, W. L. 'Cowrie shells as amulets in Europe', *Folklore*, 53, 1942

Honey, W. B. 'The work of James Giles', *English Ceramic Circle Transactions*, 1973

Lane, A. and Charleston, R. J. 'Girl in a Swing porcelain and Chelsea', *English Ceramic Circle Transactions*, 1962

Launert, E. 'Scent and scent bottles', *Antique Dealer and Collector's Guide*, August and September 1971

—— 'Scent bottles', *The Glass Circle*, No. 1, 58–64, 1972

Lehmann, K. 'The dome of heaven', *Art Bulletin*, No. 27, 1–27, 1945

Mariacher, G. 'I Lattimi dei Miotti al Museo Vetrario di Murano', *Bolletino dei Musei Civici Venetiani*, Vol. II, 1958

Pichter, E. 'Riechschnecke als Pestschutzamulet', *Deutsche Gaue*, 1952

Polak, Ada. 'Sulphides and medals', *Journal of Glass Studies*, No. 8, 1966

Tate, H. 'An anonymous loan to the British Museum of Renaissance jewellery', *The Connoisseur*, November 1963

Turner, W. 'Silver and plated ware: pomanders', *The Connoisseur*, March 1912

Wenham, E. 'Pomanders', *The Connoisseur*, April 1934

Index